BEST AIKIDO

BEST AIKIDO
The Fundamentals

Kisshomaru Ueshiba
Moriteru Ueshiba

Translated by John Stevens

KODANSHA INTERNATIONAL
Tokyo•New York•London

For information concerning the Aikikai Foundation,
please refer to the below:

Aikido World Headquarters
Aikikai Foundation

17-18 Wakamatsu-cho
Shinjuku-ku, Tokyo
162-0056 Japan
Tel: 81-(0)3-3203-9236
Fax: 81-(0)3-3204-8145
Website: www.aikikai.or.jp
E-mail: aikido@aikikai.or.jp

Front Jacket photo by Naoto Suzuki.

Originally published in Japanese as *Kihan Aikido: Kihon-hen* by Aikikai
and Shuppan Geijutsu-sha in 1997.

Distributed in the United States by Kodansha America, Inc., 575 Lexington
Avenue, New York, N.Y. 10022, and in the United Kingdom and continen-
tal Europe by Kodansha Europe Ltd., 95 Aldwych, London WC2B 4JF.

Published by Kodansha International Ltd., 17-14 Otowa 1-chome, Bunkyo-
ku, Tokyo 112-8652, and Kodansha America, Inc. Copyright © 2002
Kisshomaru Ueshiba, Moriteru Ueshiba and Kodansha International Ltd.
Translation © 2002 John Stevens. All rights reserved. Printed in Japan.

ISBN 4-7700-2762-1
First edition, 2002
02 03 04 05 06 07 08 09 10   10 9 8 7 6 5 4 3 2 1

www.thejapanpage.com

CONTENTS

Foreword 9

What Is Aikido? 10

Aikido Questions and Answers 14

CHAPTER ONE
PREPARATION FOR TRAINING 20

1. Stance (*Kamae*) 22
2. Combative Distance and Eye Focus (*Ma-ai* and *Me-tsuke*) 23
3. Etiquette, Formal Sitting, Knee Walking (*Rei, Zaho, Shikko*) 24
4. Foot Movement (*Unsoku*) 28

   Basic Step (*Ayumi Ashi*) 28

   Continuous Step (*Tsugi Ashi*) 29

   Sending Step (*Okuri Ashi*) 29
5. Body Movement (*Sabaki*) 30

   Irimi (Entering) (against a punch) 30

   Irimi (against a *jo* attack) 30

   Tenkan (Pivot Turn) 30

   Katate-dori Tenkan (Body Turn when held by one wrist) 32

   Tenshin (Sweeping Body Turn) 33

   Tenkai (Revolving Turn) 34
6. Breakfalls (*Ukemi*) 36

   Back Breakfall (*Ushiro hanten ukemi*) 36

   Front Breakfall (*Zenpo kaiten ukemi*) 38

   Full Back Breakfall (*Koho kaiten ukemi*) 38

   Pinning Technique Breakfall (*Katame waza ukemi*) 41

   Side Breakfall (*Yoko ukemi*) 42
7. Hand-Sword (*Te-gatana*) 43
8. Warm-up Exercises for the Wrist (*Tekubi Kansetsu Junan Ho*) 44

   Kote-mawashi ho 44

   Kote-gaeshi ho 45
9. Back Stretch (*Haishin Undo*) 45
10. Body Turn (*Tai no Tenkan*) 46

    Shiho-giri (*Omote*) 46

    Shiho-giri (*Ura*) 48

CHAPTER TWO
FUNDAMENTAL TECHNIQUES 50

THROWING TECHNIQUES (*NAGE-WAZA*) 51

1. *Irimi-nage* (Entering Throw) 51

   Katate-dori Irimi-nage (*ai-hanmi*) 52

   Shomen-uchi Irimi-nage 52
2. *Shiho-nage* (Four-Directions Throw) 54

   Katate-dori Shiho-nage (*ai-hanmi*) (*omote*) 54

   Katate-dori Shiho-nage (*ai-hanmi*) (*ura*) 54

   Katate-dori Shiho-nage (*gyaku-hanmi*) (*omote*) 56

   Katate-dori Shiho-nage (*gyaku-hanmi*) (*ura*) 56

PINNING TECHNIQUES (*KATAME-WAZA*) 58

1. *Dai-Ikkyo* (Pin Number One)

   Katate-dori Dai-Ikkyo (*ai-hanmi*) (*omote*) 58

   Katate-dori Dai-Ikkyo (*ai-hanmi*) (*ura*) 58

   Shomen-uchi Dai-Ikkyo (*omote*) 60

   Shomen-uchi Dai-Ikkyo (*ura*) 60

   Shomen-uchi Dai-Ikkyo (*suwari-waza*) (*omote*) 62

   Shomen-uchi Dai-Ikkyo (*suwari-waza*) (*ura*) 62

KOKYU-HO (BREATH POWER TRAINING) 64

   Standing (*rippo*) (*omote*) 64

   Standing (*rippo*) (*ura*) 66

   Sitting (*za-ho*) 68

   Tenchi-nage and Breath Power 70

CHAPTER THREE
BASIC TECHNIQUES 71

THROWING TECHNIQUES (*NAGE-WAZA*) 72

1. *Irimi-nage* 72

   Yokomen-uchi Irimi-nage 72

   Katate-dori Irimi-nage (*gyaku-hanmi*) (*irimi*) 74

   Katate-dori Irimi-nage (*gyaku-hanmi*) (*tenkan*) 74

   Tsuki Irimi-nage (*irimi*) 76

Tsuki Irimi-nage (tenshin) 76

Ushiro Ryotekubi-dori Irimi-nage 78

2. *Shiho-nage*

Yokomen-uchi Shiho-nage (omote) 80

Yokomen-uchi Shiho-nage (ura) 82

Ryote-dori Shiho-nage (omote) 84

Ryote-dori Shiho-nage (ura) 84

Hanmi-hantachi Katate-dori Shiho-nage (omote) 86

Hanmi-hantachi Katate-dori Shiho-nage (ura) 86

Ushiro Ryotekubi-dori Shiho-nage (omote) 89

Ushiro Ryotekubi-dori Shiho-nage (ura) 91

3. *Tenchi-nage* 92

Tenchi-nage (omote) 92

Tenchi-nage (ura) 92

4. *Kaiten-nage* 94

Katate-dori Kaiten-nage (uchi-kaiten) 94

Katate-dori Kaiten-nage (soto-kaiten) 94

Tsuki Kaiten-nage 96

Ushiro Ryotekubi-dori Kaiten-nage 96

THROWING AND PINNING COMBINATION TECHNIQUES (*NAGE-KATAME WAZA*) 98

1. *Kote-gaeshi* 98

Shomen-uchi Kote-gaeshi 98

Yokomen-uchi Kote-gaeshi 100

Tsuki Kote-gaeshi (irimi) 102

Tsuki Kote-gaeshi (tenshin) 104

Katate-dori Kote-gaeshi (gyaku-hanmi) 106

Ushiro Ryotekubi-dori Kote-gaeshi 108

PINNING TECHNIQUES (*KATAME-WAZA*) 110

1. *Dai-Ikkyo (Ude-osae)* (Arm Pin) 110

Katate-dori Dai-Ikkyo (gyaku-hanmi) (omote) 110

Katate-dori Dai-Ikkyo (gyaku-hanmi) (ura) 112

Kata-dori Dai-Ikkyo (omote) 115

Kata-dori Dai-Ikkyo (ura) 117

Ushiro Ryotekubi-dori Dai-Ikkyo (omote) 119

Ushiro Ryotekubi-dori Dai-Ikkyo (ura) 121

2. *Dai-Nikyo (Kote-mawashi)* (Wrist Turn) 122

Shomen-uchi Dai-Nikyo (omote) 122

Shomen-uchi Dai-Nikyo (ura) 125

Kata-dori Dai-Nikyo (suwari-waza) (seated) *(omote)* 127

Kata-dori Dai-Nikyo (suwari-waza) (seated) *(ura)* 128

Katate-dori Dai-Nikyo (gyaku-hanmi) (omote) 131

Katate-dori Dai-Nikyo (gyaku-hanmi) (ura) 132

Ushiro Ryotekubi-dori Dai-Nikyo (omote) 134

Ushiro Ryotekubi-dori Dai-Nikyo (ura) 137

3. *Dai-Sankyo (Kote-hineri)* (Wrist Twist) 138

Shomen-uchi Dai-Sankyo (suwari-waza) (seated) *(omote)* 138

Shomen-uchi Dai-Sankyo (suwari-waza) (seated) *(ura)* 140

Katate-dori Dai-Sankyo (gyaku-hanmi) (omote: uchi-kaiten) 142

Katate-dori Dai-Sankyo (gyaku-hanmi) (ura: uchi-kaiten) 145

Ushiro Ryotekubi-dori Dai-Sankyo (omote) 147

Ushiro Ryotekubi-dori Dai-Sankyo (ura) 149

4. *Dai-Yonkyo (Tekubi-osae)* (Wrist Pin) 150

Shomen-uchi Dai-Yonkyo (omote) 150

Shomen-uchi Dai-Yonkyo (ura) 150

Katate-dori Dai-Yonkyo (gyaku-hanmi) (omote) 153

Katate-dori Dai-Yonkyo (gyaku-hanmi) (ura) 155

Ushiro Ryotekubi-dori Dai-Yonkyo (omote) 157

Ushiro Ryotekubi-dori Dai-Yonkyo (ura) 158

5. *Dai-Gokyo (Ude-nobashi)* (Arm Extension) 160

Shomen-uchi Dai-Gokyo (omote) 160

Shomen-uchi Dai-Gokyo (ura) 162

Yokomen-uchi Dai-Gokyo (omote) 164

Yokomen-uchi Dai-Gokyo (ura) 166

The late Kisshomaru Ueshiba and his son Moriteru Ueshiba, Doshu, standing before a relief of Morihei Ueshiba, the Founder of Aikido, at the Headquarters Dojo.

FOREWORD

Best Aikido was written for the following reasons: Although it is a difficult concept for beginning students to understand, the techniques of Aikido are born from the harmonization between the human body and the universal energy (*ki*) of heaven and earth. Or more simply, all the various Aikido techniques are derived from the principle of natural movement. Since each and every Aikido technique has a special character, open to individual interpretation, the number of Aikido techniques is limitless. Thus, Aikido cannot be taught in strictly set patterns or put into a rigid system. This has been the approach to Aikido instruction since the art was established by the Founder, Morihei Ueshiba.

I received direct instruction from the Founder for many years, and thereafter worked in accordance with his wishes to promote Aikido. Aikido is now an art practiced internationally by millions of men and women, young and old, in many countries.

In order to establish the practice of Aikido even more widely, after careful consideration I selected, from the vast number of possibilities, the techniques most essential to the art. These techniques can be practiced by anyone, young or old, and will make it easier to train and achieve efficiency in the art.

Furthermore, Aikido contains many important principles as a martial art. It is my belief that these principles have universal validity, and the spirit behind Aikido techniques should be even more widely disseminated.

This book is not merely a technical manual. Such manuals only describe the outer form of Aikido. In this book, Aikido is presented as a spiritual path as well as a martial art. *Best Aikido* contains the essentials for understanding the art, the essentials for training, and the essential forms of Aikido.

I am pleased that this primer, *Best Aikido*, was co-authored with my son Moriteru, who is carrying on the tradition of developing and promoting Aikido, according to its true principles. We are entering a new era, and I welcome his full participation in the creation of the text and posing for the photographs demonstrating the techniques. It is my sincere hope that this book will aid all practitioners of the art in their further understanding of the form and spirit of Aikido, and facilitate their training.

August, 1997
Kisshomaru Ueshiba

WHAT IS AIKIDO?

Those who are not well informed about the true character of Aikido consider it to be nothing more than one of the old-fashioned martial arts. It is true that Morihei Ueshiba (1883–1969), the Founder of Aikido, studied many different kinds of traditional martial arts, and used that experience to formulate the techniques of Aikido. However, Aikido is far more than a composite of various martial arts. The Founder made that very clear: "Heretofore, I studied many kinds of martial art systems—Yagyu Ryu, Shinyo Ryu, Kito Ryu, Daito Ryu, Shinkage Ryu, and so on—but Aikido is not a composite of those arts. All Aiki techniques are a function of *ki*."

Nevertheless, Aikido and Daito Ryu Aikijutsu are often confused even in Japanese reference works, and it is easy to understand why the general public cannot easily distinguish between the two arts. It is a fact that Morihei Ueshiba was once a disciple of Sokaku Takeda (1859–1943), Grandmaster of the Daito Ryu, but when he was asked by a newspaper reporter if the creation of Aikido was a direct consequence of his training in the Daito Ryu, Morihei replied "No. It is more accurate to say that Master Sokaku opened my eyes to the true nature of Budo." The essential nature of Aikido is quite different from the other martial arts.

The traditional martial arts of Japan can be considered important cultural and historical treasures, but after the Meiji Restoration in 1868, and the collapse of the old samurai order, the rapid and often indiscriminate westernization of the country had a deleterious effect on all the martial arts. Jigoro Kano (1860–1938) believed that the best elements of the Japanese martial arts should be preserved but it was very difficult for him to find and learn from accom-plished masters—most of the old-time martial artists had disappeared. It was only through diligent and sustained effort that he was able to establish Kodokan Judo as a vehicle to preserve the best of the traditional Japanese martial arts in a modern context. Kano opened his first school in 1882, one year before Morihei Ueshiba was born. While Kano believed that introducing western style sports competition would help popularize his new art of Judo, Morihei followed a completely different path. So different in fact, that some people say, "Aikido is not really a martial art, is it?"

Again, it is true that there are a number of poorly informed people who mistakenly view Aikido as some kind of health promoting exercise, a kind of dance, a form of martial mesmerism, or some such thing, and, as we mentioned earlier, even reference works confuse Aikido and Aikijutsu. Let it be clear, however, that Aikido is Budo, a martial art. Aikido is a refinement of traditional martial techniques combined with an exalted philosophy of the spirit. It is a method of forging mind and body.

What is the exact nature of that philosophy of the spirit? To state it simply, it is the avoidance of the use of trickery, deception, or brute force to defeat an opponent. It is a vehicle to help us in our search for the Way, and it enables us to develop our individual character in a mutually satisfying manner with our training partners. In our search for the Way, we need to unify mind and body in order to harmonize ourselves with the natural order of the universe, and then respond freely to any contingency that may arise. Aikido is a training system that provides us the means to actually experience such a state.

The word "universe" is usually thought of as

some overwhelmingly grand concept, but actually the universe of the Way of Aikido is very concrete and centered within one's own body. In Aikido training, we strive to understand the principles of *ki* through actual experience and employ various techniques to make those principles part of our everyday consciousness. This is one of the distinctive characteristics of Aikido.

Let us look more closely at the nature of *ki* in Aikido in a concrete manner. When you see Aikido techniques performed, it is best to view all the movements as circular. When a circle is created, one's partner seems to spin off and fall of his own accord. Circular movements allow us to avoid collision with an opposing force, and facilitate harmonization. In order to create a true circle, there must be a firm center.

All of the movements in Aikido are circular.

A spinning top revolves at a high speed around a stable center, yet hardly appears to move at all. If you touch the top slightly, however, it will immediately fly off with a burst of centrifugal force, and its latent power becomes evident.

The energy radiated by a spinning top is a perfect example of "stillness within movement."

The Founder often described the state of stillness within movement as *sumikiri*, "total clarity of mind and body." This concept lies at the very heart of Aikido.

In 1924, the Founder accompanied the Omoto-kyo religious leader Onisaburo Deguchi (1871–1947) on a mission to Mongolia. On their way through the mountains, Onisaburo and his party were attacked by bandits. Bullets rained down on them from all sides. The martial artist Morihei, who was acting as Onisaburo's bodyguard, thought that they were finished but then he suddenly felt extraordinarily calm and centered. He could sense the direction of the bullets and avoided being struck. The entire party escaped unscathed. The Founder later described that extraordinarily calm state as *sumikiri*, stillness within movement, and said after that amazing experience he could immediately perceive any murderous or hostile intent that arose from any quarter.

This miraculous episode is quite enticing but it must not be overlooked that the Founder's experience of *sumikiri* was due to his long years of daily intense training of the body and mind. It did not occur easily, with no effort. Without constant practice, understanding of the true nature of *ki* will never be attained.

In the dojo, training follows certain rules. On the street, however, anything can happen, making it difficult for us to retain our equanimity. It is easy to maintain one's equanimity under ideal circumstances; one of the goals of Aikido is to teach us how to maintain our equanimity regardless of the situation, no matter how harrowing or difficult.

One method of keeping yourself centered is to breathe from the *seika tanden* (a psychophysical point about two inches below the navel). Remind yourself that the *ki* that animates your own body is the same *ki* that animates the entire universe. All the circular movements that you practice in Aikido are never contrary to the principles of nature. Control your breath and unite yourself with the natural rhythm of the universe. This is the way to keep centered in your *seika tanden*. Your own center must be linked to the center of the earth. *Ki* emanates from that sensation of stability and calm.

Kisshomaru Ueshiba bathing himself with the rays of the morning sun while performing *ki* development exercises. (At the Aiki Shrine)

Unlike many other martial art masters who tended to formulate elaborate rules and regulations for their training halls, Morihei disliked that practice and demanded only that his disciples follow their natural common sense. However, as Aikido became more and more popular his senior students requested that he establish some kind of guideline for training. "Times have changed, it seems," Morihei responded with a smile and came up with "Precautions for Aikido Training."

1. Aikido techniques can be instantly lethal so it is essential to observe the instructor's directions at all times and not engage in contests of strength.
2. Aikido is an art in which "the one" is used to strike "the many." Train yourself to be mindful of attacks coming from four and eight directions.
3. Always train in a vibrant and joyful manner.
4. The instructor can only impart a small portion of the teaching. Only through ceaseless training can you obtain the necessary experience to bring these mysteries alive.
5. In daily training, begin with basic movements to strengthen the body without overexertion. Warm up properly, and there will be no fear of injury, even for older people. Enjoy yourself while training and strive to comprehend its true purpose.
6. The purpose of Aikido training is to forge the body and mind and to build one's character. The techniques are transmitted from person to person on an individual basis, and should not be disclosed indiscriminately to outsiders, nor used for evil purposes.

These precautions are still quietly observed at the Headquarters Dojo, with the most emphasis being placed on number three, "Always train in a vibrant and joyful manner."

At the mention of the term "martial art," many people conjure up an image of a person with an intimidating, aggressive demeanor, and indeed there are some so-called martial artists who act like that. However, such demeanor is a clear indication that one does not really understand Budo. Excessive aggression is really a vain boast masking a lack of self-confidence. One who truly understands Budo is, on the contrary, quite calm in appearance and gentle in demeanor. He or she is confident enough not to try to intimidate other human beings, and typically has a happy expression on his or her face. To put it simply, they manifest *shizen tai*, a perfectly natural and relaxed state of being. In order to help them understand this kind of natural elation, I often say to the trainees, "Shouldn't we train in a joyful manner?"

We cherish those trainees who really understand the heart of Aikido. Such trainees come to the dojo in high spirits, take pleasure in throwing and being thrown, work up a good sweat, and depart in high spirits. They are not interested in seeking a high rank—they simply delight in the joy of training. They manifest *shizen tai*, a completely natural state of being.

The smiling Founder demonstrating the principle of "Always train in a vibrant and joyful manner."

The earth was born from the universe and those who flourish in that life-giving environment can directly become one with nature. They never oppose natural law, and never try to control things through force. Such people manifest a natural and matter-of-fact equanimity.

Such an attitude, based on deep experience, can be a great plus in a variety of social activities. If you train in a natural, fulfilling manner, with equanimity and a solid center, a tremendous amount of *ki* power will be generated. That will be of great benefit to both oneself and society. This is our natural, ideal form. To achieve that state of being is of far greater value than victory in some trifling contest.

The purpose of Aikido is to make human beings strong by tapping their natural energy. This will also make them healthy in mind and body. In Aikido, we transcend the distinction between mind and body; we unify body and mind and function as a single entity. It is from the center of that unified entity that limitless *ki* is born, and vital breath springs forth. If those powerful forces are manifested in daily life, one can lead the best and most positive kind of existence.

Ki power that emerges naturally and directly enables us daily to experience the joy, power, freedom, and flexibility of existence. Living vibrantly with true vigor, we can meet any challenge and accommodate ourselves to any contingency. The practice of Aikido can make this all possible, and this emphasis on harmonization and accommodation accounts for its worldwide popularity.

AIKIDO QUESTIONS AND ANSWERS

Aikido can be difficult for modern people to understand. Many only have experience with sports and games that stress pure physical and technical training and organized competition that demands a clear distinction between winner and loser. Since the Aikido approach is not like that, newcomers to the art are often puzzled. In order to make Aikido more accessible, here we will employ a question and answer format to deal with the most common queries. Many of the replies may appear startling at first but once you take up the actual practice of Aikido, you will soon learn to appreciate its unique character.

Q: How does Aikido differ from ordinary sports?
A: Aikido is Budo. It is a special kind of martial art that stresses spiritual development.

However, it is also true that Aikido has been recognized as member of the GAISF, an international association of sports federations since 1984, so it is not inconceivable to consider Aikido to be a kind of sports-like athletic activity. It must be noted, though, that in the World Games sponsored by the GAISF there is no organized competition, and it is free of the hype and commercialism of the Olympic Games.

While sports focus entirely on competition, the primary purpose of Aikido is spiritual development of the entire human being. In Aikido, we never resort to trickery, deception, or excessive force to overcome an opponent. This is how Aikido differs from sports.

In the modern world of sports, mental management is often mentioned, but if mind control is only employed to defeat an opponent it does not really facilitate spiritual development. This is why in Japan the Ministry of Education has issued a directive for instructors not to neglect the spiritual aspect of sports education. Many educators now realize that winning is not the end all and be all of sports, and perhaps Aikido and sports will eventually come to share a somewhat similar perspective.

In conclusion, we must state again that the primary purpose of Aikido is spiritual development. It is Budo, and the art emerged from a milieu in which the matter of life and death was decided in an instant. Aikido looks at the entire human being, on the deepest level, something that sports cannot do. Aikido employs the training methods of the traditional martial arts within the context of modern society.

Q: Why are there no contests in Aikido?
A: If we think of Budo within the context of contemporary society, it is clear that it must have some other purpose than teaching people how to use martial art techniques to defeat an opponent. Who is interested in that kind of thing anymore? People are interested in doing things that have practical application to their lives. Modern Budo must have some connection with the problems of daily life. This is one reason that "In Aikido, there are no contests."

In Aikido, there is no concept of "defeating an opponent." If contests are allowed, the desire to win, and the desire to vanquish an opponent arises; that fixation makes it impossible to remain in harmony with nature. Such a fixation is in direct opposition to the natural harmony of heaven and earth. The very purpose of Aikido is to unite oneself with nature and act in a harmonious manner with all things in heaven and earth. Such a state of being is impossible to achieve in organized competition, and that is why there are no contests in Aikido.

Q: Will Aikido make me strong?
A: Aikido will make you very strong. In Aikido, we forge the mind and body through daily training. The development of spiritual strength will give you the unshakable confidence to meet any challenge. That is true strength.

Q: What is the most important factor in spiritual development?
A: Aikido is Budo. It is not mere mental training. The only way to learn is by actual experience through daily practice. It is not a simple act like chanting incantations or reading a text. It is very important to understand this.

Not to be shaken by anything, and not to lose one's center—this is the heart of Aikido instruction. In the martial arts, one is taught to keep centered by focusing on the *seika tanden*. In Aikido, the importance of the *seika tanden* is not dismissed but the concept of being centered encompasses much more—you must be centered from the *seika tanden* to the bottom of your feet, you must be centered with the earth, and you must be centered and linked with the core of the universe. If you can do this, you will be able to comprehend the cosmic nature of all things.

Q: I've heard that anyone can practice Aikido—men and women, young and old. Is that true?
A: As we mentioned above, modern people are looking for things that have practical application to their daily lives. What use is an activity that can only be done when you are young, or only if you are male? Aikido can be practiced by anyone—male, female, children, the elderly. In Japan, the present male/female ratio in the martial arts is 1:3, and with the exception of Naginata, Aikido has the most women practitioners. Also, the average age of Aikido practitioners is higher than most other martial arts.

Practitioners are mainly between the ages of 18 and 40.

Aikido is based on natural movements so there is no undue stress on the body. It does not require great physical strength and thus can be practiced by anyone who has the will to train.

Anyone—male, female, young, old—can practice Aikido.

Q: Is physical conditioning such as weight training necessary for Aikido?
A: No. The Founder was quite proud of his tremendous physical strength until he encountered the Master Sokaku Takeda. Master Sokaku was a tiny, thin man, then in his fifties, but he downed Morihei with ease. If your movements are natural, excessive physical strength is not necessary, and you can continue to employ Aikido techniques regardless of age.

Also, if you do weight training and body building separately from Aikido practice, there is a tendency for the muscles to bunch and tighten, thus hindering the free flow of *ki*. It is best to build your body naturally. Even if building a stronger body is not a priority, Aikido training will naturally result in giving you stronger and more flexible muscles.

Q: What is the nature of *ki* in Aikido? Is it the same as the *ch'i* employed in the Chinese martial arts?

A: Once again, we can explain the concept in words but if one does not have any actual experience the reply will have little meaning. If you don't practice, what you have in your head is of little value.

To be sure, the concept of *ki* is central to Aikido, and the Founder always emphasized the importance of *ki.* However, the Founder's explanation of *ki* was profound and difficult to comprehend, especially for people of the modern generation. Some tried to follow what he had to say but others were not that interested in the problem. Or on occasion, the Founder would talk all about *ki* and then suddenly say with a smile, "It comes directly from the gods!"

There are various ways to interpret the concept of *ki* but those who practice Aikido sincerely will gradually develop an intuitive understanding of the real nature of *ki.* If we were to ask an Aikido practitioner about this, a likely answer would be: "When I polish the mind and body, my entire being feels vibrant!"

However, if we were to explain it to new students like this, "*Ki* is a form of enlightenment; sparks radiate from your belly and pierce the entire universe!" who would believe it? It is best to develop your own understanding of *ki* through daily training.

Regarding the relationship between *ki* and *ch'i:* They are similar but they're applied differently. The concept of *ki* is, of course, not limited to Aikido, and many martial art and philosophical systems use the term to express the notion of "universal energy" or "life force." There are many points in common between Aikido and the Chinese martial arts but the respective approach is different, and we should not consider them identical. They should be appreciated as two separate and independent systems.

Q: In Aikido, "breath power" (*kokyu-ryoku*) is emphasized. Is that related to lung capacity?

A: Aikido breath power is much more than lung capacity. It involves utilization of the entire body. It is not simply breath, but the concentrated power that arises when body and mind are unified. Breath power is crucial for Aikido. Even if one's lung capacity is not increased, one can still attain great and liberating power through unification of body and mind. Breath power and *ki* are the source of Aikido strength.

There are no human beings who do not breathe, and everyone does it unconsciously. If breathing ceases, we will quickly depart from this world. Breathing is the most natural of reflexes. *Ki* and breath power are indivisible, the very being of Aikido.

Q: When I watch people practicing Aikido, they seem to spin around like tops. Can such movements really be effective as martial art techniques?

A: In reply, let us employ the example of school education. If students only study for questions that appear on entrance exams, their education will be inadequate and incomplete. In any field of endeavor, is it possible to ignore the basics? On the contrary, master the basics and progress will come quickly.

Another approach is to teach in set patterns. In the martial arts, this would be "If that occurs, react like this." This appears to facilitate learning but in fact it is of little help in a real situation. It is impossible to postulate a set response for every contingency, and, in a real situation, you do not have the option of dictating to your opponent what kind of attack he should use.

Let's look at Aikido training methods more closely. We practice seated techniques that have no practical application in modern society—everyone sits in chairs nowadays—but training in such techniques helps you develop strong legs and hips, a solid center, and good breath power. It is not possible for every movement to have a practical application, but training in the basics will eventually give you the ability to

Moriteru Ueshiba demonstrating the subtle relationship between *ki* power and circular movements.

make an appropriate response in a real situation.

Furthermore, powerful *ki* is generated by circular movements. In order to draw a beautiful circle, it is necessary to have a true center. *Ki* emerges from that center, and it is a source of powerful revolution. If you are even slightly off-center all your power will dissipate, but if you remain on center you can slide around the strongest opposing force. This is a key principle.

The physical movements of Aikido are centered in the *seika tanden*, the middle of the human body. If you are centered in that one point, you can move in circle, small or large, with true stability and generate great *ki* power. Aikido practitioners are never just "spinning around."

Q: Are kicks used in Aikido?
A: No. The Founder had very powerful legs, and on occasion he demonstrated kicking techniques during a demonstration but almost none of those techniques were incorporated into modern Aikido.

As we have mentioned several times, Aikido emphasizes being centered in mind and body, with both feet on the ground, literally and figuratively. Kicks or leg sweeps temporarily hamper that good balance and are thus avoided.

Aikido techniques are not put into set patterns, and there is no "If that happens, do this" kind of instruction. We do not usually practice defenses against kicking attacks in Aikido, and many may view that approach as problematic, but in fact if one has a solid foundation in the basics, any kind of attack can be dealt with.

Here is an example. An Aikido instructor in Thailand was challenged by a local kick boxer. Even though the instructor tried to explain that there were no contests in Aikido, the challenger insisted. He launched a kicking attack that the Aikido instructor immediately countered. He then pinned the boxer with the *ikkyo* technique. The instructor, who had never trained against kicks, was quite surprised himself how naturally and effectively he had responded. He had no preconceived notion of how to respond so he just reacted naturally, and this reaction was due to his daily training in the Aikido basics.

Q: Is there free-style sparring (*randori*) in Aikido?
A: No, for the same reason there are no contests. We never attack first in Aikido, and only move in response to an opponent's aggression, so two Aikido practitioners would not be able to spar. However, we do have a kind of free-style training where one's partner uses a variety of attacks and one is then free to use any Aikido technique.

Q: During Aikido training how much should we resist against the application of a technique? If we resist too much it makes it difficult for a partner to train, and if we do not resist at all, what is the meaning?

A: You should not resist unduly. Many martial arts will not agree with this approach but it is not a matter of passively executing the techniques. It is a matter of cooperation, and by working with a partner you will learn to gauge how much pressure (and resistance) to apply. This is effective training.

Here is an illustration of how effective Aikido training can be. The wrestler Ichiro Yata once visited our dojo. Yata, who had been a competitor in the 1932 Los Angeles Olympics and served as chairman of the All-Japan Amateur Wrestling Association, was in good shape and an experienced wrestler, but he was completely stymied when the Aikido *nikyo* pin was applied to his wrist. Since he had no Aikido training, he was unable to resist despite all of his physical conditioning. Aikido looks easy but once you begin training you realize how much forging is necessary to build a powerful technique.

If you believe that harmonizing your movements with your partner has no value in an actual situation, and that by resisting you make the technique more realistic, you are overlooking the essential characteristic of Aikido.

Q: About how many techniques are there in Aikido?
A: At present in the Headquarters Dojo there are about 50 fundamental and basic techniques. However, once these basic movements are mastered and the principles of Aikido understood, the number of various applications is limitless. Aikido techniques are not learned externally by merely copying the movements. Just as it is impossible to fit everyone into the same mold, techniques emerge freely from within the wide-ranging Aiki movements.

Q: What is the difference between "fundamental techniques" and "basic techniques"?
A: The fundamental techniques are primary. If we draw a parallel with mathematics, the fundamental techniques would be akin to the Five Principles of Euclid. Those fundamental princi-ples are the basis of applied geometry. Since the fundamental techniques are like maxims, there are no movements in Aikido that violate those principles. Basic techniques are those techniques deduced from the fundamental techniques, and during training the proof of the maxims is clearly demonstrated.

There are those who like to make up their own maxims, but this is not possible in Budo. All the movements have to follow natural principles, and cannot be artificially constructed.

Here is an example: If you drop a stone it will fall to earth because of gravity, and that principle can never be challenged. It is a maxim that must be observed, and once that is understood as a base it can be utilized. From that fundamental maxim, the basic movements emerge, and from the basic movements variations spring forth.

Q: Isn't it a problem to remember so many techniques?
A: There are those who want to memorize every technique from the start, or have everything explained to them first before they try it. If you think like that, however, it will be very difficult to learn by following the natural flow of Aikido movements, and unifying body and mind. Excessive thinking will impede your progress. When someone says, "I cannot remember the techniques I have been taught. What should I do?" the reply is, "It is all right to forget. It is important to forget about your head, and learn directly from your body."

Q: Are there different schools of Aikido?
A: To be sure, there are many systems that claim to be "such-and-such Aikido," even without really knowing what Aikido is. And there are some splinter groups that have been established by former students of the Founder, with a few even going so far as to introduce organized competition, something that is totally contrary to the spirit of Aikido. Regardless of how similar the techniques appear, if they are divorced from the spirit of the Founder it is not Aikido.

We do not like to think that there are separate schools of Aikido. If we draw too many distinctions between different interpretations of the techniques, the universal character of Aikido will be degraded.

Q: What is the purpose of such preliminary practices as *furitama* and *torifune-undo*?
A: Those practices are forms of *misogi*, a traditional Shinto ritual for purifying the spirit and body. The Founder was deeply interested in esoteric Shinto, especially *kototama*, the science of sacred sounds, and he also studied *misogi* under the Shinto shaman Bonji Kawazura (1862–1929). The Founder engaged in such esoteric practices both before and after WWII, and some of his disciples emulated his example.

To put it simply, *misogi* is a method of puri-

The Founder and Kisshomaru Ueshiba in prayer preparing to perform *misogi* in a waterfall.

fying the body and spirit. It is hard to see how such simple movements can transform one's character, but if one practices the *misogi* ritual sincerely, it will undoubtedly have an effect.

Q: What is the Aikido approach to etiquette?
A: Etiquette is a human creation, and it is found nowhere else in the animal kingdom. The notion of what is "proper" etiquette varies greatly from culture to culture, and it is impossible to state that one particular standard of behavior is the correct one. The Aikido approach is to let a sense of etiquette develop naturally, through regular training, and there are no elaborate rules of etiquette at the Headquarters Dojo.

Here is an example: children training at an Aikido dojo in Hawaii were never told to put their shoes in order before stepping onto the mat. However, after a few months, even the messiest of the children were arranging their shoes neatly, something that greatly surprised (and pleased) their parents. The children naturally came to realize the importance of etiquette without being told by the instructor.

Any kind of etiquette that has to be rigidly enforced, is not true etiquette. "Budo training begins and ends with respect" is a common saying but even this does not have to be expressly stated. In Aikido, the best etiquette is the one that is most natural.

Q: What is the most important relationship between Aikido training and everyday life?
A: One must, for example, maintain good Aikido posture and movement throughout the day. More important, however, is to maintain a modest attitude, and harmonize mind and body. In the realm of human relationships, one must avoid conflict and resolve problems in a harmonious Aikido fashion. In order to do this well, one must above all be modest and humble.

CHAPTER ONE

Preparation for Training

Hidari-hanmi

Migi-hanmi

Preparation for Training

Prior to actual practice with a training partner, one needs a basic knowledge of Aikido concepts and terminology. Here are the fundamentals of Aikido training.

1. STANCE (*KAMAE*)

In Aikido, it is necessary to assume the proper "attitude" (another meaning of *kamae*) physically, mentally, and spiritually. When facing an opponent, one always assumes an oblique, half-body stance (*hanmi*). When the left foot is forward, it is called *hidari-hanmi* ① and when the right foot is forward, it is called *migi-hanmi* ②. When the *tori* (the one executing the technique) has his right foot forward and the *uke* (the one receiving the technique) has his left foot forward, it is called *migi-gyaku* (right-reverse) *hanmi* ③. In the opposite case, it is called *hidari-gyaku* (left-reverse) *hanmi* ④. When both partners have the same foot forward, it is called, respectively, *hidari-ai* (left-mutual) *hanmi* ⑤ and *migi-ai* (right-mutual) *hanmi* ⑥.

Migi-gyaku-hanmi   *Hidari-gyaku-hanmi*

Hidari-ai-hanmi   *Migi-ai-hanmi*

2. COMBATIVE DISTANCE AND EYE FOCUS (*MA-AI* AND *ME-TSUKE*)

Combative distance: This is the space between you and your partner. As in all martial arts, the combative distance between you and your partner is very important, both physically and psychologically. In addition to assuming the proper distance in the initial stance, it is also necessary to maintain a good distance while executing the techniques.

Eye focus: The quickest way to discern your partner's intention is through his eyes. In Aikido, we do not fix our gaze on any one point but rather attempt to take in our partner's entire form.

Kisshomaru Ueshiba employing a right *hanmi* stance.

3. ETIQUETTE, FORMAL SITTING, KNEE WALKING (*REI, ZAHO, SHIKKO*)

In Aikido, we are always careful to respect our training partners, and we express this respect with a formal bow (①, ②).

Kisshomaru Ueshiba performing the Aikido formal bow.

The essence of Aikido is to unite ourselves with the universe's energy (*ki*) and to follow the dynamic flow of nature. This is the key to all Aikido training, and this principle should be firmly implanted in every practitioner's mind. There are not a lot of rules and regulations in Aikido because we believe that by following the principles of nature one will naturally behave properly. When one is engaged in such a discipline as Aikido, it is natural to display respect by lowering one's head. From an Aikido perspective, the simple act of bowing contains and maintains all the rules necessary. Anyone, young or old, Japanese or non-Japanese, who observes simple, good etiquette will be refreshed and make good progress with their Aikido technique. Morihei Ueshiba, the Founder of Aikido, always stressed the importance of etiquette and respect in Aikido training.

How to sit

① – ③ Step backward slightly on the left foot, and drop down on the right knee.

④ Bring the left knee down next to the right knee.

⑤ Remain on the toes while lowering the hips.

⑥ – ⑦ Fold the legs under the buttocks and lower yourself into the formal sitting position (*seiza*).

How to stand

①–③ From *seiza* stand on the toes.

④–⑤ Step forward with the left foot.

⑥–⑧ Stand up in one decisive movement.

Knee Walking (*Shikko*)

①–② From *seiza* stand on the toes.

   ③ Slide forward with the left knee.

④–⑤ Slide the right foot next to the left foot.

⑥–⑦ Slide forward on the right knee.

⑧–⑨ Slide the left foot next to the right, and continue the same pattern. Knee walking is used
when practicing seated techniques (*suwari
waza*).

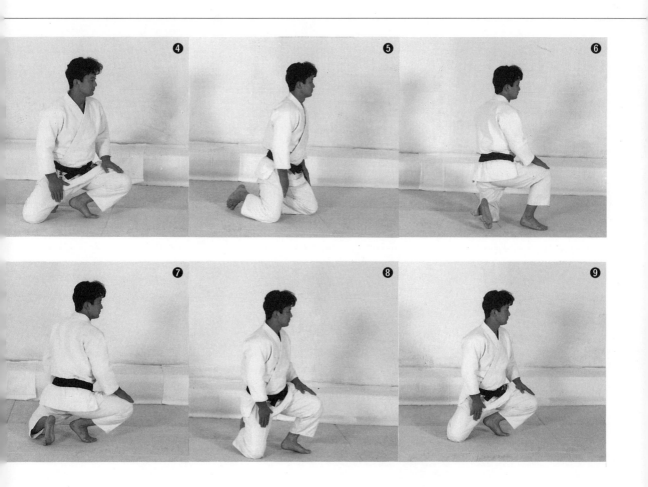

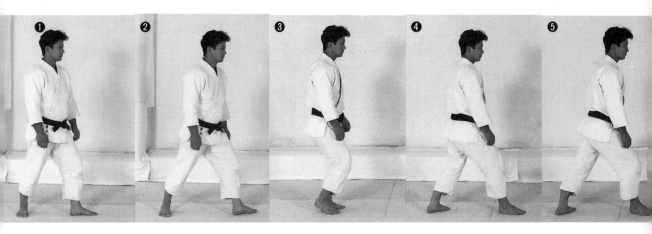

4. FOOT MOVEMENT (*UNSOKU*)

In order to move smoothly, it is necessary to keep the knees flexible, the body centered, and to use a sliding step (*suri ashi*).

Basic Step (*Ayumi Ashi*)

Keep the body centered and move forward with a sliding step, alternating the feet.

Basic Step *(Ayumi Ashi)*

Continuous Step (*Tsugi Ashi*)

From a *hanmi* stance, bring the back foot up close to the front foot, and then step forward on the front foot. Remain in the same *hanmi* stance while moving forward.

Sending Step (*Okuri Ashi*)

Step forward with the front foot and bring the back foot up, remaining in a *hanmi* stance.

Continuous Step *(Tsugi Ashi)*

Sending Step *(Okuri Ashi)*

5. BODY MOVEMENT (*SABAKI*)

In order to properly control an opponent's attack, it is essential to know how to move one's body into an advantageous position. Good body movement can be fostered by both individual and partner exercises.

Irimi (**Entering**) (against a punch)
① Assume *hidari-ai-hanmi* stance.
② *Uke* steps forward on the right foot and delivers a punch with his right fist.
③ *Tori* slides forward to the outside of the attacking thrust, and controls the opponent's arm with his left hand-sword (*te-gatana*).

Irimi (against a *jo* attack)
① Assume a *migi-gyaku-hanmi* stance.
②–③ *Tori* avoids the *jo* attack by entering to the outside while simultaneously delivering an *atemi* to *uke*'s side.

When attacking, the *uke* should move forward with full force. (*Atemi* is a preemptive strike directed toward an opponent's vital points; *atemi* is employed to put an opponent off balance or to prevent a counterattack.)

Tenkan (**Pivot Turn**) (individual practice)
①–⑤ From *hidari-hanmi* step forward on the left foot, pivot 180 degrees and resume *hidari-hanmi*.

If the coordination between the body turn and the position of the hand-swords is not good, you will find yourself relying on pure physical strength to try to move your partner.

A body turn made with the feet in the same position is called *hanten*.

Katate-dori Tenkan
(Body turn when held by one wrist)
① Assume a *migi-gyaku-hanmi* stance.

②–③ *Uke* grabs *tori*'s right wrist with his left hand. *Tori* steps forward on his front foot to *uke*'s side.

④—⑤ *Tori* executes a 180-degree turn using his right hand-sword to lead *uke*.

By employing a body turn and keeping the hand-swords in proper position, it is possible to lead *uke* without resistance (②—④).

Tenshin (Sweeping Body Turn)

①—② From a *hidari-ai-hanmi* stance, *uke* steps forward on his right foot and delivers a strike to the side of *tori*'s head.

③—⑧ *Tori* steps forward on his right foot and makes a sweeping turn while delivering *atemi* with his right hand-sword to *uke*'s face. *Tori* uses his left hand-sword to cut down on *uke*'s right arm and neutralize the attack.

Tenkai (Revolving Turn)

①–③ From *migi-ai-hanmi*, *uke* steps forward on his left foot and grabs *tori*'s right wrist with his left hand.

④–⑤ *Tori* breaks *uke*'s posture by stepping forward on his right foot.

⑥–⑨ *Tori* steps inside *uke*'s left side with his left foot and makes a revolving turn.

Regardless of the technique being executed, it is essential to keep one's center of gravity low, the knees flexible, and the turns smooth and stable. The movement in figures ⑤–⑦ is not a ducking movement but rather a smooth, evasive revolution.

6. BREAKFALLS (*UKEMI*)

Breakfalls are employed to protect the body from harm when being thrown or pinned. Also, learning how to execute breakfalls enhances your understanding of how to apply the techniques to your partner when you act as *tori*.

Back Breakfall (*Ushiro hanten ukemi*)

①–⑤ Withdraw the back leg and fold it as if sitting down in a chair. Roll back on the mat, taking care not to let the head strike the ground.

⑥–⑫ Roll back up using both feet to resume a standing position.

It is not necessary to strike the mat hard with one's hands. In order to reduce the amount of shock the body receives keep your body as circular as possible, and be ready to initiate another movement as soon as you are on your feet.

Front Breakfall (*Zenpo kaiten ukemi*)

①–⑨ Lean all the way forward, first touching the mat with the hand, and then roll over naturally with the elbow, shoulder, back, and hips lightly touching the ground. Stand all the way up, and resume a *hanmi* stance.

Full Back Breakfall (*Koho kaiten ukemi*)

①–④ Withdraw the back leg, as if sitting in a chair, and naturally roll completely over with the buttocks, hips, back, and shoulder lightly touching the ground.

⑤–⑧ Stand straight up and resume a *hanmi* stance.

CHECKPOINT: Note how *uke* bends his knees and how he places his hand on the mat as he executes the breakfall.

Pinning Technique Breakfall
(*Katame waza ukemi*)

①–⑦ *Tori* steps forward slightly on the front foot and pushes up on *uke*'s elbow and wrist. *Tori* then takes a big step forward on the back foot while controlling *uke*'s wrist and elbow and guiding him down towards the ground.

⑧–⑩ *Tori* brings *uke* completely down by lowering his body to the mat and settling on the knees.

⑪–⑫ *Tori* pins *uke*'s right arm to the ground, aligning his body along *uke*'s arm and ribs.

Side Breakfall (*Yoko ukemi*)

①–⑦ This is a flying breakfall to the side. Use the
   inside arm to break the fall and absorb the
   shock.

7. HAND-SWORD (*TE-GATANA*)

In Aikido, *kokyu-ryoku* (breath power) is very important. The key to the development of *kokyu-ryoku* is the hand-sword. The concept of hand-sword is not limited to the hand; it includes the forearm, the inner and outer wrist, the palm, and the outer edge of the hand from the fingertips to the wrist.

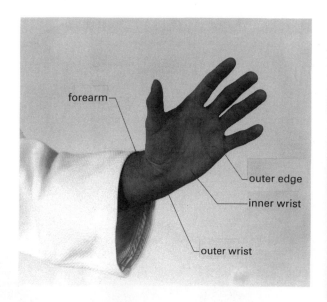

forearm

outer edge

inner wrist

outer wrist

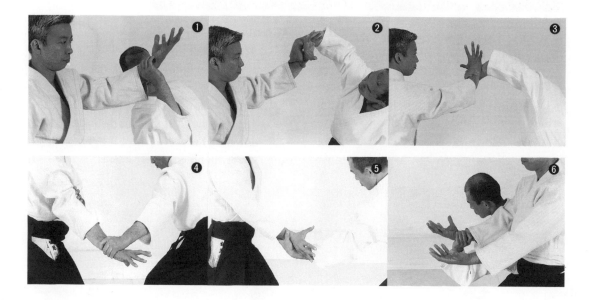

Employment of the Hand-Sword
   ① Thrusting to the partner's side.
   ② Raising and thrusting up.
   ③ Cutting up to the outside.
   ④ Cutting down to the outside.
   ⑤ Cutting down to the inside.
   ⑥ Turning the wrist in *tenkan* and leading the partner.

8. WARM-UP EXERCISES FOR THE WRIST (*TEKUBI KANSETSU JUNAN HO*)

In Aikido, many of the techniques involve control of the wrist, so it is necessary to prepare that joint prior to training. These warm-up exercises not only prepare the wrist, they also foster correct placement of the hands when executing various techniques.

Kote-mawashi ho

① Hold the left thumb with the right thumb, and the left little finger with the right little finger as shown.

② Bring the arms back toward your chest, bending the wrist towards the inside, and lowering the elbows. Repeat eight to ten times, and then change hands.

Kote-gaeshi ho

① Hold the left hand in front of the chest, with the right thumb placed between the little and ring fingers as shown.

② Twist the left hand and bring it down close to the body as shown. Repeat eight to ten times, and then change hands.

9. BACK STRETCH (*HAISHIN UNDO*)

This is a cool-down exercise at the conclusion of training.

① *Uke* grabs both of *tori*'s wrists.

②–③ Using his hand-swords, *tori* leads *uke*.

④–⑤ *Tori* aligns himself back-to-back with *uke*.

⑥ *Tori* lowers his hips and raises *uke* up off his feet as shown.

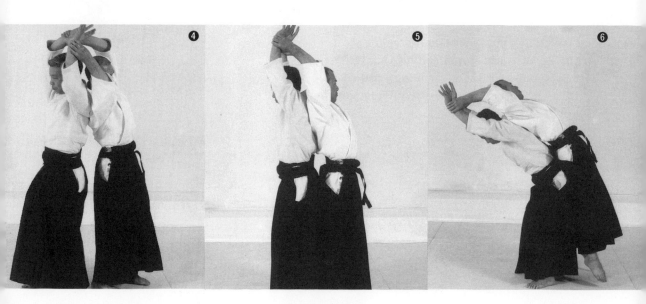

---

10. BODY TURN (*TAI NO TENKAN*)

This exercise is actually the *shiho-nage* technique without the concluding throw to the ground.

Shiho-giri (*Omote*)

① Assume the *migi-ai-hanmi* stance.
② *Uke* grabs *tori*'s wrists.
③ *Tori* steps forward slightly while raising his hand-swords.
④ *Tori* steps forward with his left foot.
⑤ *Tori* turns his body and cuts down with his hand-swords.
⑥–⑦ *Tori* stops halfway through and stretches *uke* out.

When *tori* moves forward in front of *uke* it is termed an *omote* (front) technique; when *tori* moves to the outside of *uke* it is termed an *ura* (back) technique. (See next page.) It is important to move the hand-swords slowly in big motions when guiding *uke*.

Figures ③–⑧ shows the sweeping step and big *kaiten* turn used to control *uke* and break his posture.

Shiho-giri (Ura)

① Assume a *migi-gyaku-hanmi* stance.

② *Uke* grabs *tori*'s wrists.

③ *Tori* steps forward on his front foot and pivots 180 degrees.

④ *Tori* raises both hand-swords while shifting his center.

⑤ *Tori* cuts down with both hand-swords.

⑥–⑦ *Tori* stops halfway and stretches *uke* out.

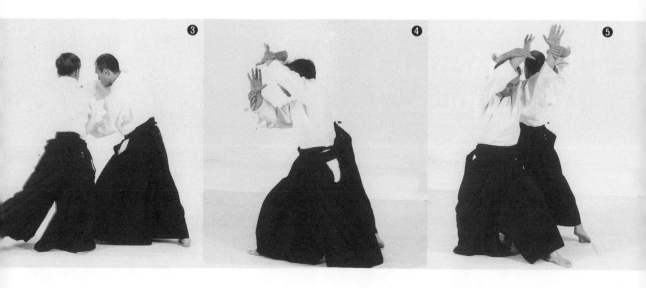

❸ ❹ ❺

If the cut is followed through like this, the exercise becomes a *shiho-nage* throw.

49

CHAPTER TWO

Fundamental Techniques

There are a number of fundamental techniques essential for the proper practice of Aikido. Aikido techniques are generally described as being either *omote* (front) or *ura* (back). In *omote* techniques, the movements are based on the principle of entering, and in *ura* techniques, the movements are based on the principle of turning. The techniques are always practiced on both sides, so the technical directions given in this book are reversed when starting from the opposite side. As mentioned earlier, *tori* is the one who executes the technique; *uke* is the one who receives the technique.

Katate-dori Irimi-nage (ai-hanmi)
① Assume a *migi-ai-hanmi* stance.

THROWING TECHNIQUES (*NAGE-WAZA*)

1. *IRIMI-NAGE* (ENTERING THROW)

In *irimi-nage* you first avoid the attack by entering deeply to the side of your partner and positioning yourself in his dead spot (at the point where he can offer no resistance). Then you keep yourself centered while using your partner's force to move him, and then break his posture to down him with a throw. The principle of entering is common to many Aikido techniques and *irimi-nage* is one of the keys to mastering Aikido.

Shomen-uchi Irimi-nage
① Assume a *migi-ai-hanmi* stance.

Katate-dori Irimi-nage (ai-hanmi) (continued from p. 51)

② *Uke* grabs *tori*'s right wrist with his right hand.

③ *Tori* takes a big step forward with his left foot and gets completely behind *uke*. (If the entry is not deep enough you will be unable to break your partner's posture.)

④–⑤ *Tori* pivots on his left foot, while holding *uke*'s neck.

⑥ When *uke* attempts to rise, *tori* guides him with his right shoulder.

⑦–⑧ *Tori* takes a big step forward on his right foot, forms an arc with his right arm, breaks *uke*'s posture, and downs him.

Shomen-uchi Irimi-nage (continued from p. 51)

② *Uke* steps forward on the right foot and delivers a *shomen* attack with his right hand-sword.

③ *Tori* enters and reaches for *uke*'s neck with his left hand.

④–⑤ *Tori* pivots on the left foot and breaks *uke*'s posture.

⑥ When *uke* attempts to rise, *tori* guides him with his right shoulder.

⑦–⑨ *Tori* steps forward on his right foot, forms an arc with his right arm, and cuts down to bring *uke* to the ground.

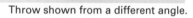

Throw shown from a different angle.

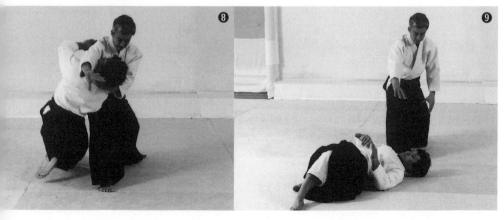

2. *SHIHO-NAGE* (FOUR-DIRECTIONS THROW)

In *shiho-nage* both the feet and the hands are employed to cut in four or eight directions. The movements in *shiho-nage* are based on the principle of the sword, another key aspect of Aikido techniques. Constant practice of *shiho-nage* naturally provides a solid base for all other techniques.

Katate-dori Shiho-nage (ai-hanmi)

(*omote*)

① Assume a *migi-ai-hanmi* stance.
② *Uke* grabs *tori's* right wrist with his right hand.
③ *Tori* opens to the right with his right foot and grabs *uke's* right wrist with his right hand.
④—⑥ *Tori* steps forward with his left foot, grabs *uke's* arm with both hands, and then pivots with both feet. *Tori* takes a step forward with his right foot while cutting down with both hands to bring *uke* to the ground.

Katate-dori Shiho-nage (ai-hanmi)

(*ura*)

① Assume a *hidari-ai-hanmi* stance.
② *Uke* grabs *tori's* left wrist with his left hand.
③—④ Using his hand-sword to guide *uke, tori* steps in with his right foot to *uke's* left side, and grabs *uke's* arm with both hands.
⑤—⑥ *Tori* pivots on both feet, and then takes a step forward on his left foot while cutting down with both hands to bring *uke* to the ground.

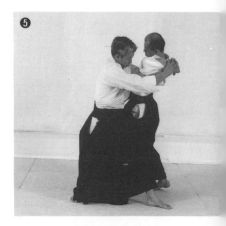

In ③–⑤ *uke*'s arm is not pulled but is rather controlled with a big step in on the left foot and a clean pivot, making it possible to throw him without resistance.

When executing the throw, cut down while taking a big step forward and it will be easy to break *uke*'s posture and throw him.

Katate-dori Shiho-nage (gyaku-hanmi) (omote)

① Assume a *hidari-gyaku-hanmi* stance.

② *Uke* grabs *tori*'s left wrist with his right hand.

③–⑤ *Tori* takes a step forward slightly to the right with his right foot, concentrating all of his breath power in his left hand-sword, and then raises his hands in a spiraling motion.

⑥–⑧ After completing a big step forward with his left foot, *tori* pivots on his right foot, steps forward, and cuts down to accomplish the throw.

Katate-dori Shiho-nage (gyaku-hanmi) (ura)

① Assume a *migi-gyaku-hanmi* stance.

② *Uke* grabs *tori*'s right wrist with his left hand.

③–④ *Tori* steps forward on his right foot to *uke*'s left side and begins to pivot while taking hold of *uke*'s left arm with both hands.

⑤ *Tori* pivots on both feet.

⑥–⑦ *Tori* steps forward on his left foot and cuts down to complete the throw.

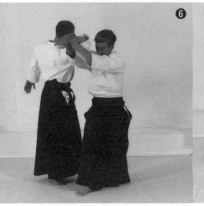

PINNING TECHNIQUES (*KATAME-WAZA*)

1. *DAI-IKKYO* (PIN NUMBER ONE)

Dai-Ikkyo is the basis of all the pinning techniques in Aikido, and it is essential for beginning students to develop a solid understanding of its execution.

Katate-dori Dai-Ikkyo (ai-hanmi) (*omote*)

① Assume a *migi-ai-hanmi* stance.
② When *uke* grabs *tori*'s right wrist with his right hand, *tori* immediately employs his hand-sword.
③ *Tori* opens to the right, keeping his right hand-sword in front of his own center, and holds *uke*'s right elbow with his left hand.
④ *Tori* takes a big step forward on his right foot, grabs *uke*'s wrist and elbow, and cuts down in an arc.
⑤–⑥ *Tori* brings *uke* down by cutting all the way to the ground. He plants his left knee first and then sits on both knees to bring *uke* under complete control as shown, holding *uke*'s wrist, extending his arm, and keeping the left knee against his ribs.

Katate-dori Dai-Ikkyo (ai-hanmi) (*ura*)

① Assume a *migi-ai-hanmi* stance.
② *Uke* grabs *tori*'s right wrist with his right hand.
③ *Tori* raises his right hand-sword in a spiraling motion and grabs *uke*'s right elbow.
④–⑤ *Tori* steps forward on his left foot and makes a sweeping pivot while controlling *uke*'s elbow and wrist. He brings *uke* face down to the ground and pins him as shown.

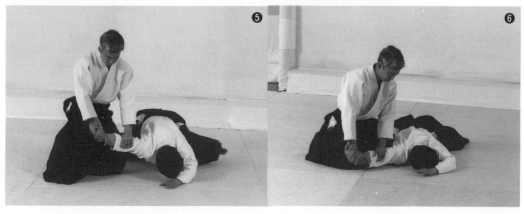

Shomen-uchi Dai-Ikkyo (omote)

① Assume a *migi-ai-hanmi* stance.

② *Uke* steps forward and delivers a *shomen* strike with his right hand-sword.

③ *Tori* controls *uke*'s right elbow with his left hand and moves his right hand-sword into position to grab *uke*'s right wrist.

④ *Tori* takes a big step forward with his left foot while cutting down on *uke*'s right arm.

⑤ *Tori* continues to move forward, bringing *uke* to the ground by controlling his right arm.

⑥ By maintaining the proper posture, *tori* pins *uke* face down on the ground.

Shomen-uchi Dai-Ikkyo (ura)

① Assume a *migi-ai-hanmi* stance.

②–③ *Uke* steps forward and delivers a *shomen* strike with his right hand-sword.

④ *Tori* steps forward on his left foot, grabs *uke*'s right elbow with his left hand, and moves his right hand-sword into position to control *uke*'s right wrist.

⑤–⑥ *Tori* makes a big pivot while cutting down on *uke*'s arm and brings him to the ground.

⑦ *Tori* puts *uke* under complete control with the *ikkyo* pin.

CHECKPOINT: When pinning your partner use your little fingers to apply full pressure.

Shomen-uchi Dai-Ikkyo (suwari-waza)

(*omote*)

① Sit in *seiza* as shown.

② *Uke* moves forward on his right knee to deliver a *shomen* strike with his right hand-sword.

③ *Tori* controls the attack by grabbing *uke*'s right elbow and wrist.

④–⑤ *Tori* steps forward with his left foot and cuts down forcefully on *uke*'s right arm.

⑥–⑦ *Tori* slides forward and brings *uke* under complete control by pinning his elbow and wrist as shown.

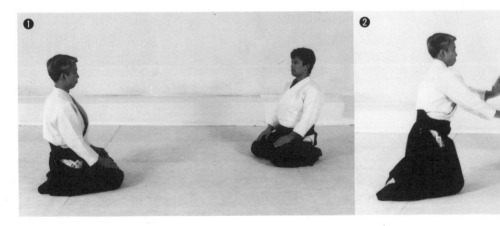

Shomen-uchi Dai-Ikkyo (suwari-waza)

(*ura*)

① Sit in *seiza*.

② *Uke* steps forward to deliver a *shomen* strike with his left hand-sword.

③ *Tori* slides forward on his right knee to *uke*'s left side and grabs his elbow and wrist.

④ *Tori* pivots on the right knee while cutting down on *uke*'s arm.

⑤ *Tori* brings *uke* under complete control and pins him as shown.

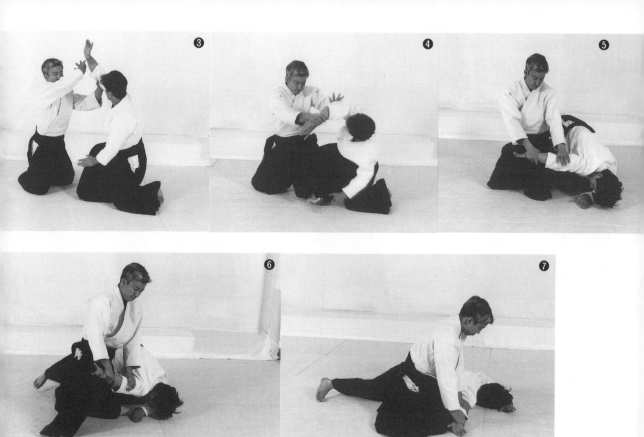

In the *ura* pinning movement, do not try to pull your partner down. Instead use a good entering movement and a full turn to bring him down without undue resistance.

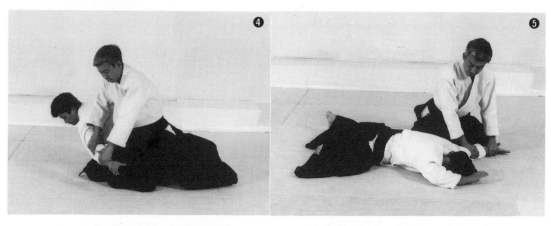

KOKYU-HO (BREATH POWER TRAINING)

The utilization of concentrated power is called *kokyu-ryoku* (breath power). In Aikido, the concept of "breath" is not limited to the nose and mouth; it encompasses the entire body, every pore of the skin, and it originates in the power of nature. *Kokyu* also has the meaning of "proper timing." There are several exercises in Aikido designed to foster breath power, and they are practiced both sitting and standing.

Standing (*rippo*)
(*omote*)

① Assume a *hidari-ai-hanmi* stance.

②–③ *Uke* uses his left hand-sword to cut down on *tori*'s left arm and then grabs that arm with both hands.

④ *Tori* takes a step forward on his right foot and puts full breath power into his left-hand sword.

⑤ *Tori* steps behind *uke* with his left foot and raises his left arm.

⑥–⑦ *Tori* completes the step in with his left foot while cutting down with both hands to down *uke*.

In ③ and ④, the hand-sword is kept in front
of one's center. In ⑤, the arm is also raised from
one's center while the back foot slides behind one's
partner and breaks his posture, making it possible
to throw him without resistance (as in figure ⑦).

Practical application of *kokyu* power as seen in
morote-kokyu-nage.

Standing (rippo)

(ura)

① Assume a *hidari-ai-hanmi* stance.

②–③ *Uke* uses his left hand-sword to cut down on *tori*'s left arm, and then grabs that arm with both hands.

④–⑤ *Tori* steps to *uke*'s side with his left foot and pivots, using his left hand-sword to guide *uke* up and break his posture.

⑥–⑦ *Tori* takes a big step back on his left foot and cuts down with both arms, bringing *uke* to the ground.

Kokyu-ho is designed to help you develop your *ki* (life force). In the example here, the hand that is grabbed is kept in front of one's own center, thus facilitating smooth, unhindered movement. This type of movement has many practical applications in Aikido techniques.

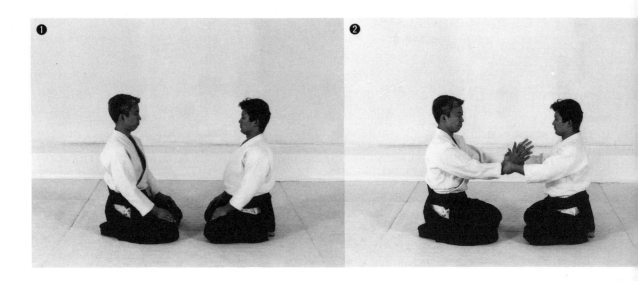

Sitting *(za-ho)*

① Sit in *seiza*.

② *Uke* grabs *tori*'s wrists from the outside.

③ *Tori* uses his hand-swords to raise *uke*'s arms.

④ *Tori* slides forward on the right knee as he cuts down with both hands.

⑤ *Tori* cuts all the way down to *uke*'s left bringing him to the ground.

⑧ *Tori* uses both hand-swords to pin *uke*.

Here the breath power hand-swords are employed in an *ushiro ryotekubi-dori* technique.

Proper hand-sword position in Figure ④,
shown from the front.

CHECKPOINT: Concentrate your power in your hand-swords but do not push your partner. Raise his arms, and he will not be able to use any strength against you. Then he can be thrown by simply moving forward.

Tenchi-nage and Breath Power

The effective, concentrated use of power is one of the distinctive characteristics of Aikido. Look at this photograph of *tenchi-nage* (heaven-and-earth throw) to see how such power is employed. *Tori*'s right hand-sword is splayed upwards from his center toward heaven, and his left hand-sword, with power concentrated in the little finger, is extended toward earth. The effectiveness of both hand-swords is clearly evident. *Uke*'s arms are spread wide apart, negating his power, and his balance is broken. *Tori* has taken a big step forward with his right foot and will cut down with both hands to complete the throw.

Breath power training is the key to good Aikido movement. In this book, the standing technique *(rippo)* requires that you place your arms close to your body, concentrate your power in your hand-sword, and keep your hand-sword in front of your own center. In the seated technique *(za-ho)*, use your hand-swords to raise *uke*'s arms and break his posture. When these breath power methods are properly employed it is possible to execute such a technique as *tenchi-nage*. The practice of *kokyu-ho* leads to the development of *kokyu-ryoku* and fosters an appreciation of the importance of *ki*, the essential life force.

CHAPTER THREE

Basic Techniques

The basic techniques flesh out the fundamental techniques with a variety of applications, depending on the type of attack. Master the basic techniques and you will naturally be able to apply them in any number of situations.

THROWING TECHNIQUES (*NAGE-WAZA*)

1. *IRIMI-NAGE*

Yokomen-uchi Irimi-nage

① Assume a *hidari-ai-hanmi* stance.

② *Uke* steps forward on his right foot and delivers a *yokomen* strike with his right hand-sword.

③–④ *Tori* steps in on his right foot and pivots while cutting down on *uke*'s attacking arm.

⑤ *Tori* steps behind *uke* with his left foot and uses his left hand to control *uke*'s neck.

⑥–⑦ *Tori* sweeps around with his right foot and guides *uke* up.

⑧–⑨ *Tori* brings *uke*'s head against his right shoulder, steps in with his right foot, and cuts down to effect the throw.

Katate-dori Irimi-nage (gyaku-hanmi) (irimi)

① Assume a *hidari-gyaku-hanmi* stance.

②–④ *Uke* grabs *tori*'s left wrist with his right hand. *Tori* uses his right hand-sword to break the grip, and shifts to *uke*'s right side.

⑤ *Tori* steps in deeply and grabs *uke*'s neck.

⑥–⑦ *Tori* makes a big sweeping turn with his right foot, breaking *uke*'s posture.

⑧–⑨ *Tori* brings *uke*'s head against his right shoulder and steps in on his right foot while cutting down to effect the throw.

Katate-dori Irimi-nage (gyaku-hanmi) (tenkan)

① Assume a *hidari-gyaku-hanmi* stance.

②–③ *Uke* grabs *tori*'s left wrist with his right hand. *Tori* steps forward on his left foot to *uke*'s side and pivots.

④–⑤ *Tori* completes the pivot and grabs *uke*'s right wrist from underneath to release *uke*'s grip. *Tori* holds *uke*'s wrist and reaches for his neck.

⑥–⑦ *Tori* takes hold of *uke*'s neck and makes a big sweep to the right, breaking his posture.

⑧ *Tori* brings *uke*'s head under control next to his right shoulder.

⑨ *Tori* steps in on his right foot and cuts down, effecting the throw.

Tsuki Irimi-nage

(irimi)

① Assume a *hidari-ai-hanmi* stance.

② *Uke* steps forward on his right foot and delivers a punch with his right fist.

③ *Tori* steps forward to *uke*'s right side, using his left hand-sword to deflect the blow.

④ *Tori* brings *uke*'s head under control with his right shoulder.

⑤–⑦ *Tori* takes a big step forward with his right foot and cuts down with his right arm to effect the throw.

When applying the throw do not rely on arm power alone. Use the movement of your entire body to break your partner's posture.

Tsuki Irimi-nage

(tenshin)

① Assume a *hidari-ai-hanmi* stance.

②–③ *Uke* steps forward on his right foot to deliver a punch with his right fist. *Tori* steps forward on his right foot and deflects the blow with his right hand.

④ *Tori* steps forward on his left foot and enters behind *uke*.

⑤ *Tori* sweeps behind *uke* with his right foot and breaks his posture.

⑥ *Tori* brings *uke*'s head under control with his right shoulder.

⑦–⑧ *Tori* steps forward on his right foot while cutting down with his right arm to effect the throw.

Ushiro Ryotekubi-dori Irimi-nage

① Assume a *migi-ai-hanmi* stance.

②–④ From the front, *uke* moves around to *tori*'s rear and grabs both his wrists. When his wrists are grabbed, *tori* takes one step forward on his left foot.

⑤ *Tori* raises both hands in a big motion.

⑥ *Tori* takes a slight step back to the left with his left leg and enters behind *uke*.

⑦–⑧ *Tori* grabs *uke*'s neck with his left hand and pivots on his left foot, breaking *uke*'s posture.

⑨–⑪ *Tori* brings *uke*'s head under control with his right shoulder, and steps forward on his right foot while cutting down with his right arm to effect the throw.

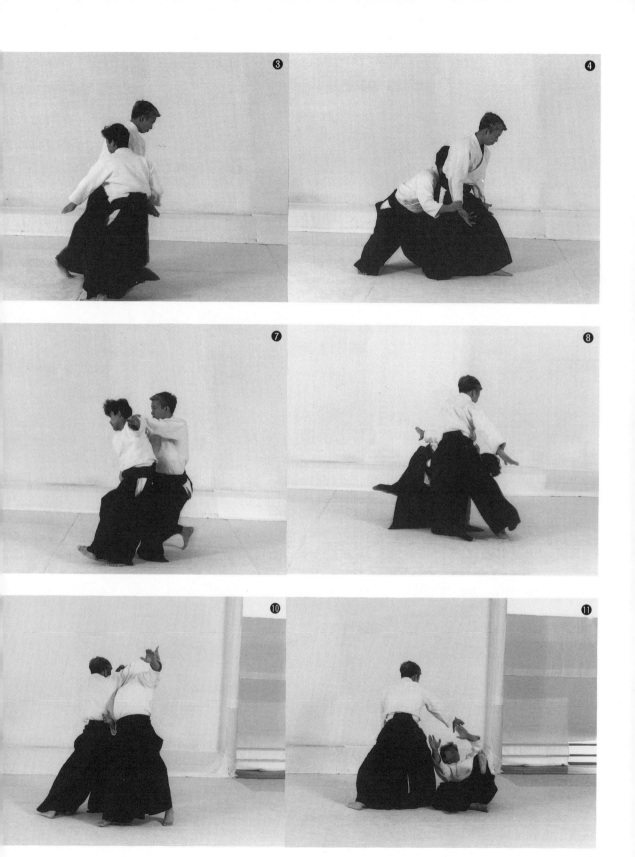

2. SHIHO-NAGE

Yokomen-uchi Shiho-nage

(*omote*)

① Assume a *hidari-ai-hanmi* stance.

② *Uke* delivers a *yokomen* strike with his right hand-sword and *tori* steps forward on his right foot.

③–④ *Tori* steps forward on his right foot and turns inward while deflecting *uke*'s attack and simultaneously applying *atemi* to *uke*'s face with his right hand-sword. *Tori* then cuts down on *uke*'s attacking arm.

⑤ *Tori* holds *uke*'s right wrist with his right hand, turning it out away from his body.

⑥ *Tori* takes a big step forward, holds *uke*'s arm with both hands, and starts to pivot.

⑦–⑧ *Tori* completes the pivot and cuts down with both hands while taking a step forward on his right foot to effect the throw.

CHECKPOINT: Use the little finger of your right hand to keep a tight grip and place your left hand on top to further secure control of your partner's arm; cut down as if holding a sword.

Close-up of figure ⑦.

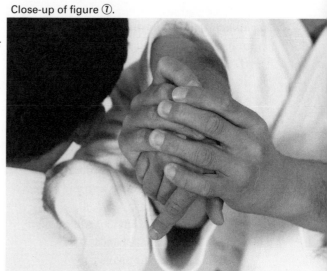

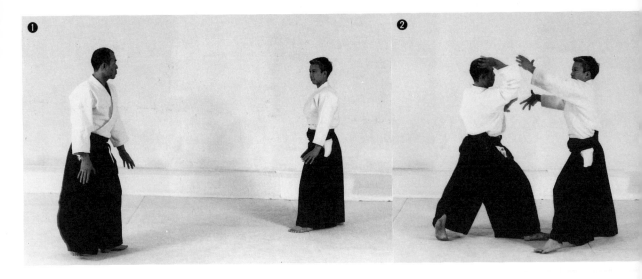

Yokomen-uchi Shiho-nage

(*ura*)

① Assume a *hidari-ai-hanmi* stance.

② *Uke* delivers a *yokomen* strike with his right hand-sword and *tori* brings his left foot forward, to *uke*'s right.

③ *Tori* controls the attack, using his left hand-sword to deflect the blow and his right hand-sword to apply *atemi*.

④ *Tori* cuts down on *uke*'s arm and grabs his right wrist.

⑤ *Tori* pivots on the left foot while holding *uke*'s arm with both hands.

⑥ *Tori* completes the pivot.

⑦ *Tori* steps forward on his right foot and cuts down to effect the throw.

In ④–⑧ do not pull on *uke*'s arm. Rather, use a full body turn to bring his arm around and then step forward to break his posture.

❸

❹

❻

❼

CHECKPOINT: Cover your right hand with your left hand, and use the thumb and index finger of your right hand to get a good grip on your partner's hand; tighten the grip further with your little fingers.

Close-up of figure ❻.

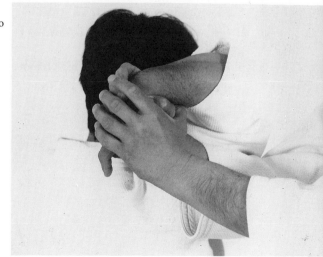

Ryote-dori Shiho-nage

(*omote*)

① Assume a *migi-ai-hanmi* stance.

② *Uke* steps forward and grabs *tori*'s wrists.

③ *Tori* grabs *uke*'s right wrist while stepping forward on his right foot.

④ *Tori* steps forward on his left foot, raising his hands over his head, and then pivots.

⑤–⑥ *Tori* completes the pivot, holds *uke*'s arm in both hands, and cuts down while taking a step forward on his right foot.

Ryote-dori Shiho-nage

(*ura*)

① Assume a *migi-gyaku-hanmi* stance.

② *Uke* steps forward and grabs *tori*'s wrists.

③ *Tori* steps forward on his right foot to *uke*'s left side.

④ *Tori* pivots on his right foot and holds *uke*'s left wrist with his left hand.

⑤ *Tori* completes the pivot and cuts down with both hands.

⑥–⑦ *Tori* takes a step forward with his left foot and effects the throw.

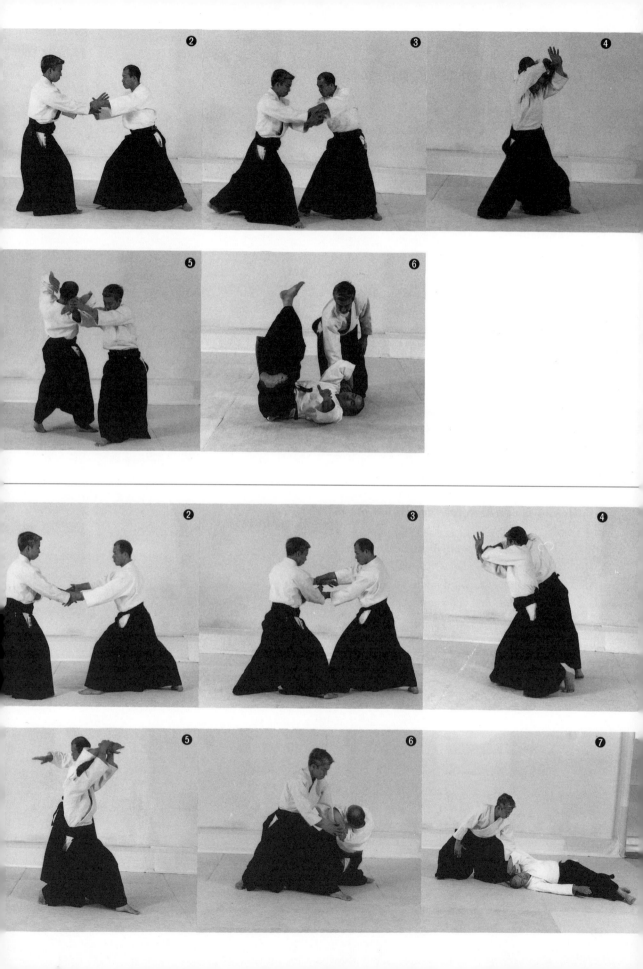

Hanmi-hantachi Katate-dori Shiho-nage
(*omote*)

① *Uke* approaches *tori* from the left diagonal.
② *Uke* grabs *tori*'s left wrist with his right hand.
③ *Tori* steps forward with his left foot and grabs *uke*'s right wrist.
④ *Tori* pivots and cuts down.
⑤–⑧ *Tori* takes a step forward on his right foot and ends the throw with an arm pin.

Do not pull on your partner's arm when making the throw. Use a good body turn made on your knees to render the technique effective.

Hanmi-hantachi Katate-dori Shiho-nage
(*ura*)

① *Uke* approaches *tori* from the left diagonal.
② *Uke* grabs *tori*'s left wrist with his right hand.
③–⑤ *Tori* moves forward on his left foot to *uke*'s right side, and grabs *uke*'s right wrist with his right hand.
⑥ *Tori* pivots and cuts down.
⑦–⑧ *Tori* slides forward and ends the throw with an arm pin.

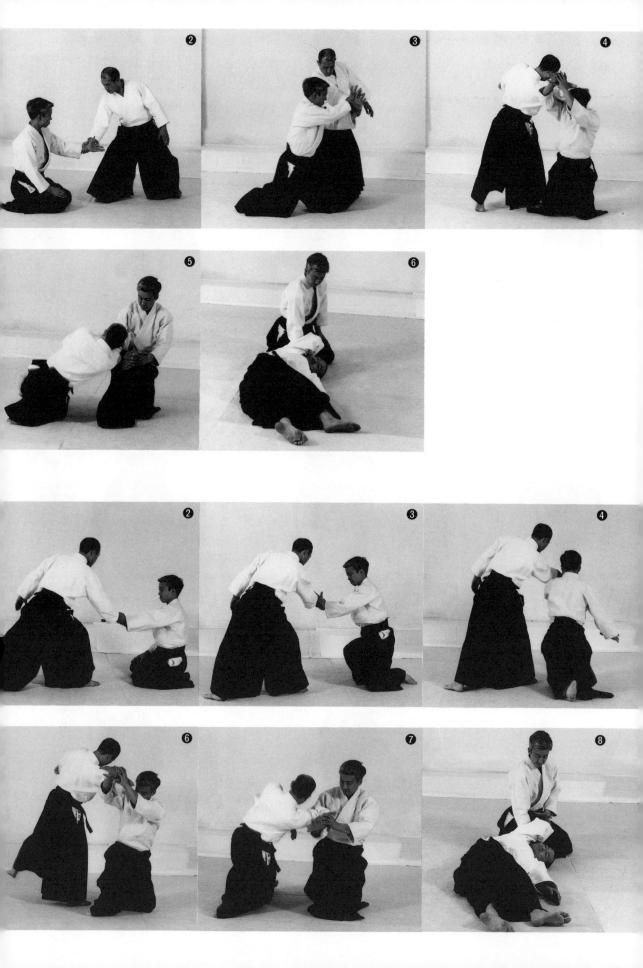

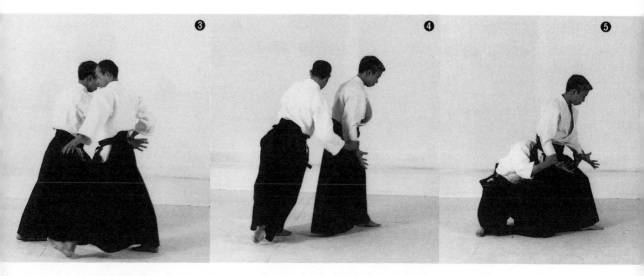

Ushiro Ryotekubi-dori Shiho-nage
(*omote*)

① Assume a *migi-ai-hanmi* stance.

②–⑤ *Uke* approaches from the front, cuts down on *tori*'s right wrist with his right hand-sword, moves behind *tori*, and grabs *tori*'s wrists. When his wrists are grabbed from behind, *tori* takes a slight step forward on his left foot.

⑥–⑦ *Tori* raises his arms high.

⑧ *Tori* steps back on his left foot while bringing both hands down.

⑨ *Tori* holds *uke*'s left wrist with both hands.

⑩ *Tori* steps forward on his right foot and raises *uke*'s arm.

⑪ *Tori* pivots and cuts down.

⑫ *Tori* takes a step forward and pins *uke* to the ground.

In ⑤–⑥, do not use just your arms. Keep your arms close to your body, spread your fingers widely, and keep yourself centered.

In ⑦–⑧, use your body movement to the back to break *uke*'s posture.

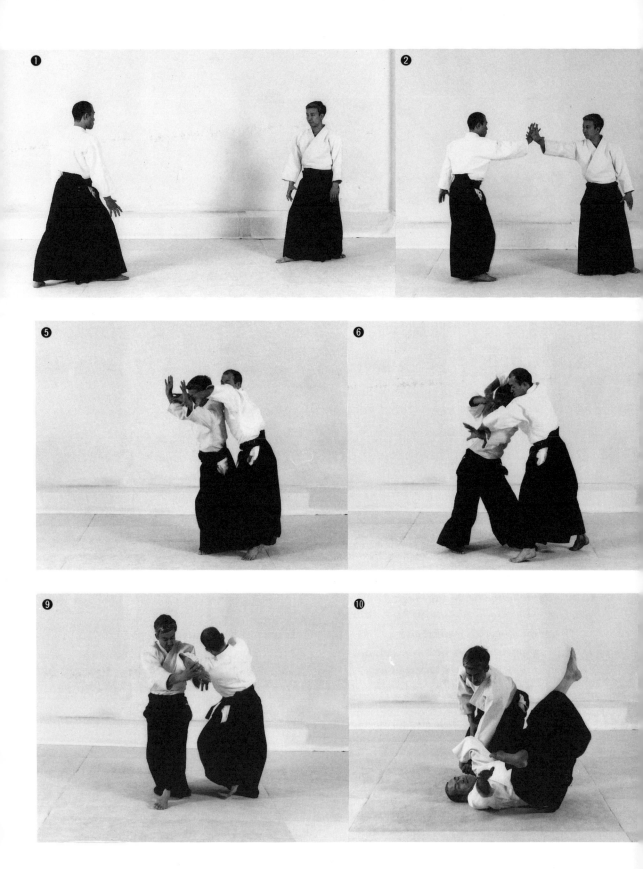

Ushiro Ryotekubi-dori Shiho-nage

(*ura*)

① Assume a *migi-ai-hanmi* stance.

②–④ *Uke* approaches from the front and moves around to grab *tori*'s wrists from behind. When *tori*'s wrists are grabbed, he takes a step forward with his left foot.

⑤ *Tori* raises his arms high.

⑥–⑦ *Tori* steps in toward *uke* on his right foot and grabs *uke*'s left wrist with both hands.

⑧ *Tori* steps to *uke*'s left side with his right foot and pivots.

⑨ *Tori* completes the pivot and cuts down.

⑩ *Tori* takes a step forward and ends the throw with a pin.

Tenchi-nage (omote)

3. TENCHI-NAGE

This technique is called *tenchi* (heaven-and-earth) *nage* because the hands are extended upward and downward to throw your partner. In order to execute *tenchi-nage* properly you must spread your fingers, unify mind, *ki*, and body to manifest your breath power, and extend your arms as if piercing heaven and earth.

Tenchi-nage

(*omote*)

   ① Assume a *migi-ai-hanmi* stance.
   ② As soon as *uke* grabs *tori*'s wrists, *tori* begins to raise his right hand-sword up toward heaven and his left hand-sword down toward earth.
   ③ *Tori* enters to *uke*'s right side.
④–⑤ *Tori* takes a big step forward on his right foot and throws *uke* to the front.

Tenchi-nage (ura)

Tenchi-nage

(*ura*)

①–③ Assume a *migi-ai-hanmi* stance. When *uke* grabs *tori*'s wrists, *tori* steps forward on his left foot to *uke*'s right side and turns, opening out.
   ④ The right hand-sword is extended up and the left hand-sword extended down.
⑤–⑥ *Tori* takes a big step forward on his right foot and throws *uke* to the front.

To throw the hand-swords, spread the fingers widely and concentrate your force in your little fingers. Make the *uke* spread his arms away from his body and break his posture. Take a big step forward and throw.

4. KAITEN-NAGE

Aikido movements are said to resemble the circular turns of a sphere. *Kaiten-nage*, in particular, is based on the principle of seamless rotation. When you step to the inside of your partner, the technique is called *uchi-kaiten*, and when you step to the outside of your partner, it is called *soto-kaiten*.

Katate-dori Kaiten-nage (uchi-kaiten)
① Assume a *migi-gyaku-hanmi* stance.
② *Uke* grabs *tori*'s right wrist with his left hand.
③ *Tori* takes a step forward on his right foot, and applies *atemi* with his left hand to *uke*'s face.
④ *Tori* takes a big step in with his left foot and turns.
⑤ *Tori* takes a big step back with his right foot while cutting down deeply with his right hand-sword.
⑥ *Tori* grabs *uke*'s left wrist with his right hand and presses down on *uke*'s head with his left hand as shown.
⑦–⑧ *Tori* takes a big step forward with his right foot and throws *uke* to the front.

Katate-dori Kaiten-nage (soto-kaiten)
① Assume a *migi-gyaku-hanmi* stance.
② *Uke* grabs *tori*'s right wrist with his left hand.
③ *Tori* steps forward on his right foot to *uke*'s left side, and applies *atemi* with his left hand.
④–⑤ *Tori* cuts up with his right hand-sword and pivots on his right leg.
⑥ *Tori* takes a big step back on his right foot while cutting down deeply with his right hand-sword.
⑦ *Tori* grabs *uke*'s left wrist with his right hand and presses down on his head with his left hand.
⑧–⑨ *Tori* takes a big step forward on his right foot and throws *uke* to the front.

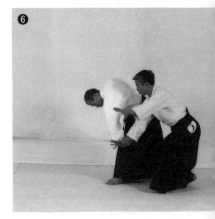

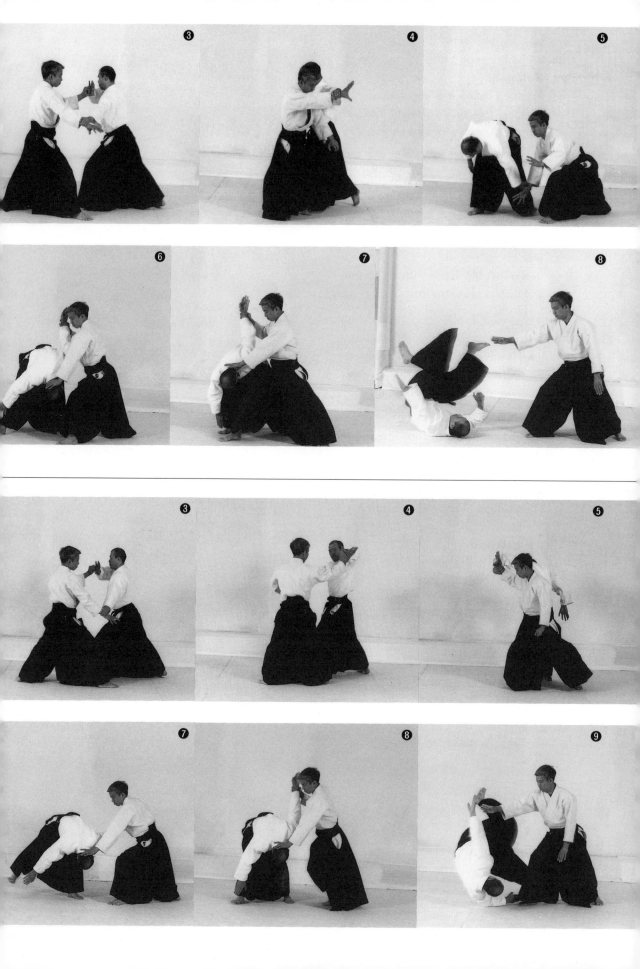

Tsuki Kaiten-nage

① Assume a *hidari-ai-hanmi* stance.

② *Uke* steps forward on his right foot and delivers a punch with his right fist. *Tori* slides forward on his left foot and deflects the blow with his left hand-sword.

③ *Tori* uses his left hand-sword to cut down on *uke*'s right arm.

④–⑤ *Tori* grabs *uke*'s right wrist with his left hand and presses down on *uke*'s neck with his right hand.

⑥–⑧ *Tori* takes a big step in with his left foot and throws *uke* to the front.

Immediately upon breaking *uke*'s balance press down firmly on the base of his skull; take a big step forward to throw him, a movement common to many Aikido techniques.

Ushiro Ryotekubi-dori Kaiten-nage

① Assume a *migi-ai-hanmi* stance.

②–④ *Uke* approaches from the front, and moves around to grab *tori*'s wrists from behind. When his wrists are grabbed, *tori* takes a step forward with his left foot.

⑤ *Tori* raises both arms.

⑥ *Tori* steps back on his left foot while cutting down with both hands.

⑦ *Tori* grabs *uke*'s right wrist with his left hand and presses down on his head with his right hand.

⑧ *Tori* takes a big step forward and throws *uke* to the front.

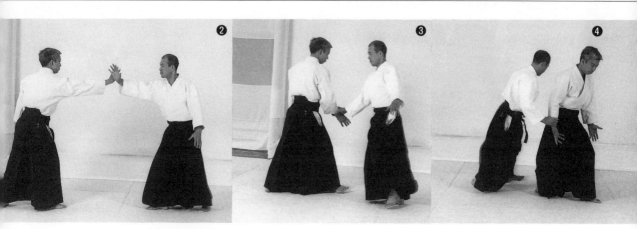

THROWING AND PINNING COMBINATION TECHNIQUES (*NAGE-KATAME WAZA*)

The combination of a throw and a finishing pin is one of the distinctive characteristics of Aikido, an example of the austere beauty of the art. After neutralizing an attack with *irimi* and good body movement, the opponent is securely pinned face down with some type of joint lock. *Kote-gaeshi* is the centerpiece of such techniques.

1. KOTE-GAESHI

This is the most representative of the throw-and-pin techniques. Your partner's hand is held in the same manner as in the *tekubi kansetsu junan ho*. When you twist his wrist to bring him down, it is important that you employ a good entry, a full turn, and sweeping body movement as well to effect the throw because a mere twist of the wrist will not suffice. After the throw, always pin your partner face down.

Shomen-uchi Kote-gaeshi

① Assume a *migi-ai-hanmi* stance.

②–③ *Uke* steps forward and delivers a *shomen* strike with his right hand-sword. *Tori* steps in to *uke*'s right side and controls *uke*'s right elbow with his left hand-sword.

④ With his left hand, *tori* applies the *kote-gaeshi* grip to *uke*'s right hand and continues his turn.

⑤ Continuing to apply the *kote-gaeshi* grip, *tori* steps back on his left foot.

⑥–⑧ *Tori* applies the *kote-gaeshi* twist with both hands, steps in with his right foot, and cuts down.

⑨–⑩ *Tori* controls *uke*'s right elbow with his right hand, pressing down until *uke* is turned over facing the ground.

⑪ *Tori* applies a pin to *uke*'s shoulder as shown.

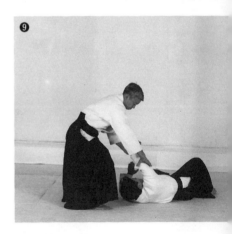

CHECKPOINT: When applying the *kote-gaeshi* grip, make sure your elbow is on the outside of your partner's elbow (close-up ④). The *kote-gaeshi* grip is applied with the thumb placed on the back of the hand between the middle and ring fingers (close-up ⑧).

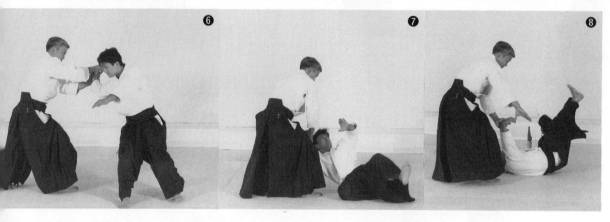

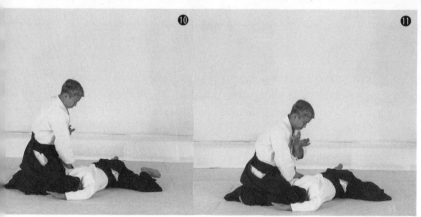

Close-up of figure ④.

Close-up of figure ⑧.

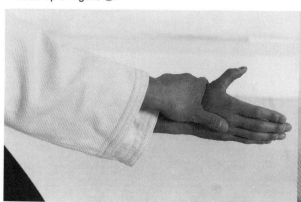

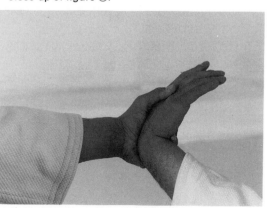

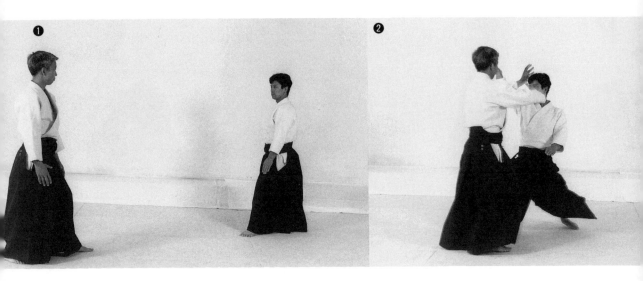

Yokomen-uchi Kote-gaeshi

① Assume a *hidari-ai-hanmi* stance.

② *Uke* steps forward on his right foot and delivers a *yokomen* strike with his right hand-sword.

③–④ *Tori* steps forward on his right foot and turns inward while cutting down on *uke*'s attacking arm.

⑤ *Tori* steps forward on his left foot and pivots while applying the *kote-gaeshi* grip to *uke*'s right hand.

⑥ *Tori* steps in to the left with his right foot.

⑦ *Tori* applies the *kote-gaeshi* twist with both hands and throws *uke* to the ground.

⑧–⑨ *Tori* holds *uke*'s wrist with his left hand and presses down on *uke*'s right elbow until *uke* turns face down to the ground.

⑩ *Tori* pins *uke*'s shoulder as shown.

In ⑥–⑦, do not rely exclusively on the wrist twist to bring your partner down. Take a big step in and use your entire body to effect the throw. In ⑩ keep your right knee against *uke*'s shoulder to pin him.

Tsuki Kote-gaeshi
(*irimi*)

① Assume a *hidari-ai-hanmi* stance.

② *Uke* steps forward with his right foot to deliver a punch with his right fist.

③ *Tori* enters to *uke*'s right side and deflects the punch with his left hand-sword.

④ *Tori* pivots on his left foot and grabs *uke*'s right wrist.

⑤ *Tori* steps in to the left with his right foot.

⑥–⑦ *Tori* applies the *kote-gaeshi* twist with both hands and throws *uke*.

⑧–⑨ *Tori* controls *uke*'s wrist and elbow and presses down until *uke* turns face down on the ground.

⑩ *Tori* applies a shoulder pin.

In ⑧–⑨, press your partner's elbow towards his head, keeping the side of his body open, making it difficult for him to offer any resistance. Then you will be able to make him turn over towards the ground.

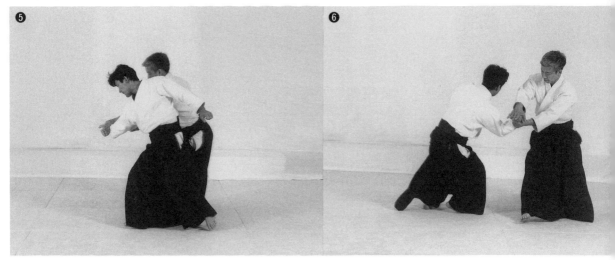

Tsuki Kote-gaeshi

(*tenshin*)

① Assume a *hidari-ai-hanmi* stance.

② *Uke* steps forward on his right foot and delivers a punch with his right fist.

③ *Tori* steps forward on his right foot to the inside and deflects *uke*'s punch with his right hand-sword.

④–⑤ *Tori* steps forward on his left foot, grabs *uke*'s right wrist, and pivots.

⑥–⑦ *Tori* steps in with his right foot while applying the *kote-gaeshi* twist and throws *uke*.

⑧–⑨ *Tori* controls *uke*'s wrist and elbow while pressing down towards his head and turns him face down on the ground.

⑩ *Tori* pins *uke*'s shoulder. In the pin, the left hand is turned upwards and the left arm held tight against his body in order to completely control *uke*'s wrist and upper arm.

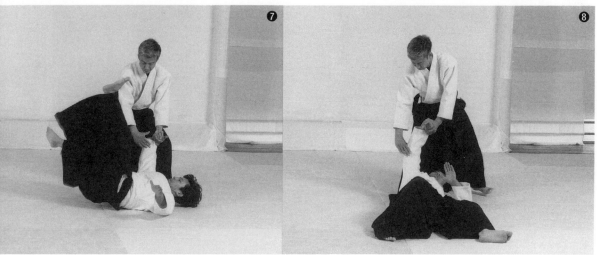

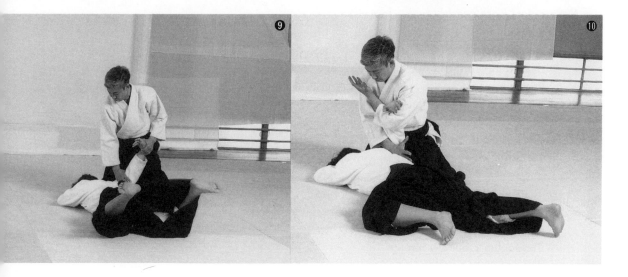

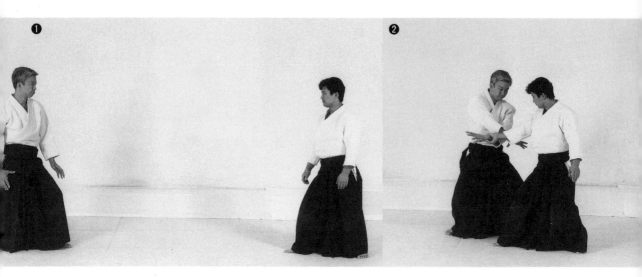

Katate-dori Kote-gaeshi (gyaku-hanmi)

① Assume a *hidari-gyaku-hanmi* stance.

② As soon as *uke* grabs *tori's* left wrist, *tori* enters to *uke's* right while cutting down with his right hand-sword to break *uke's* hold.

③ *Tori* pivots on his left foot and grabs *uke's* right wrist with his left hand.

④ *Tori* steps in to the left with his right foot.

⑤–⑥ *Tori* applies the *kote-gaeshi* twist with both hands and throws *uke*.

⑦–⑧ *Tori* controls *uke's* wrist and elbow, pressing down toward *uke's* head and turning him face down to the ground.

⑨–⑩ *Tori* applies a shoulder pin.

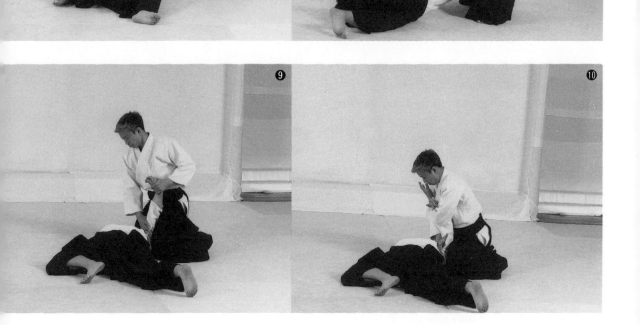

Ushiro Ryotekubi-dori Kote-gaeshi

① Assume a *migi-ai-hanmi* stance.

②–④ *Uke* approaches from the front, and then moves around to grab *tori*'s wrists from behind. When his wrists are grabbed, *tori* takes a step forward with his left foot.

⑤ *Tori* raises his arms high.

⑥ *Tori* cuts down with both hands and grabs *uke*'s left wrist with his right hand.

⑦ *Tori* pivots on his right foot.

⑧–⑨ *Tori* sweeps to the right with his left foot while applying the *kote-gaeshi* grip. *Tori* applies the *kote-gaeshi* twist with both hands to *uke*'s left wrist and throws him.

⑩–⑪ *Tori* controls *uke*'s wrist and elbow, pressing down toward his head to turn him face down to the ground, and finishes with a shoulder pin.

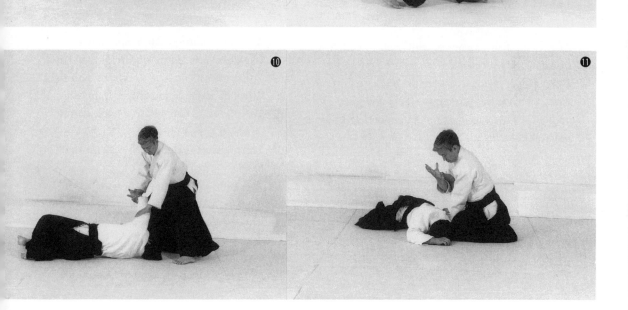

PINNING TECHNIQUES (*KATAME-WAZA*)

After neutralizing an attack with *irimi* and circular movements, your partner can be brought under control by applying a lock to his shoulder, arm, or wrist. Here we will present the locks and pins applied against *kata-dori* and *katate-dori*, in their *omote* and *ura* forms.

1. *DAI-IKKYO (UDE-OSAE)* (ARM PIN)

Katate-dori Dai-Ikkyo (gyaku-hanmi) (*omote*)

① Assume a *hidari-gyaku-hanmi* stance.

②–③ *Uke* grabs *tori*'s left wrist with his right hand.

④ *Tori* applies *atemi* to *uke*'s face with his right fist while stepping in with his right foot.

⑤–⑦ *Tori* pivots on his right foot while cutting down on *uke*'s right arm.

⑧ *Tori* grabs *uke*'s right wrist with his right hand.

⑨ *Tori* grabs *uke*'s right elbow with his left hand.

⑩–⑪ *Tori* takes two steps forward while cutting down on *uke*'s arm.

⑫–⑬ *Tori* controls *uke*'s wrist and elbow as shown and pins him face down on the ground.

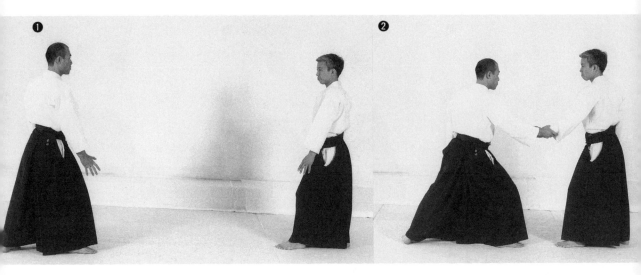

Katate-dori Dai-Ikkyo (gyaku-hanmi)

(*ura*)

① Assume a *hidari-gyaku-hanmi* stance.

② *Uke* grabs *tori*'s left wrist with his right hand.

③ *Tori* applies *atemi* to *uke*'s face with his right fist.

④ *Tori* steps out to *uke*'s right side while cutting down on *uke*'s arm with his right hand-sword.

⑤ *Tori* grabs *uke*'s right wrist with his right hand and controls *uke*'s elbow with his left hand.

⑥ *Tori* steps behind *uke* with his left foot.

⑦ *Tori* sweeps around on his right foot while cutting down on *uke*'s arm.

⑧—⑨ *Tori* controls *uke*'s elbow and wrist and pins him face down on the ground.

CHECKPOINT: When moving with your left hand-sword, place your right hand-sword on your partner's elbow to bolster control of the arm.

Close-up of figure ④

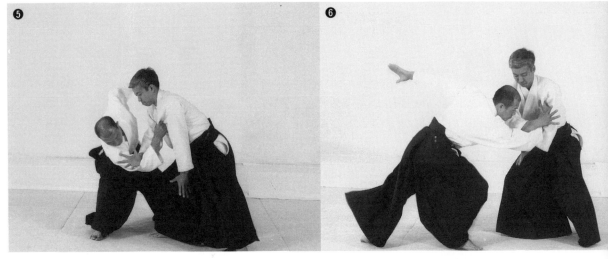

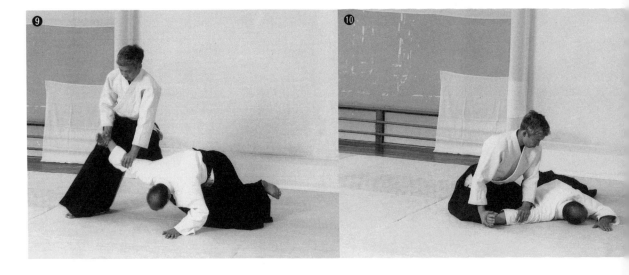

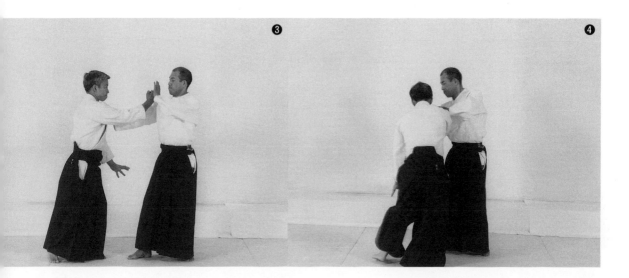

Kata-dori Dai-Ikkyo

(*omote*)

① Assume a *hidari-gyaku-hanmi* stance.

② *Uke* grabs *tori*'s left shoulder with his right hand.

③ *Tori* applies *atemi* to *uke*'s face with his right fist.

④–⑤ *Tori* steps in with his right foot while cutting down on *uke*'s right arm with his right hand-sword.

⑥ *Tori* grabs *uke*'s right wrist with his right hand.

⑦ *Tori* pushes *uke*'s right elbow up with his left hand.

⑧ *Tori* takes two big steps forward while cutting down on *uke*'s arm.

⑨–⑩ *Tori* controls *uke*'s wrist and elbow and pins him face down on the ground.

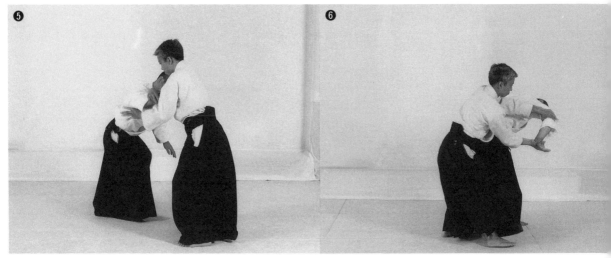

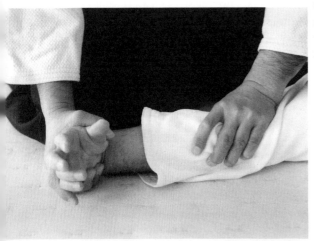

CHECKPOINT: Pin your partner's elbow by applying pressure with the little finger of your left hand, and control his wrist by applying pressure with the little finger of your right hand. Turn his wrist forward in the direction shown.

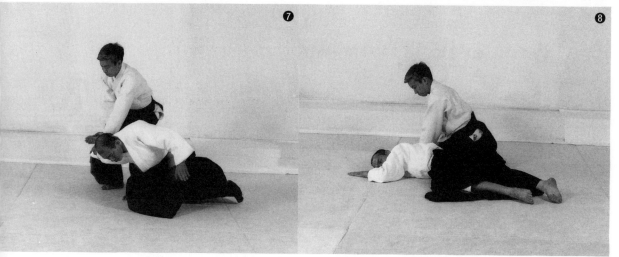

Kata-dori Dai-Ikkyo
(*ura*)

① Assume a *hidari-gyaku-hanmi* stance.
② *Uke* grabs *tori*'s left shoulder with his right hand.
③ *Tori* applies *atemi* to *uke*'s face with his right fist.
④ *Tori* steps out to *uke*'s right side while cutting down on *uke*'s right arm with his right hand-sword.

⑤ *Tori* steps in to *uke*'s right side while controlling *uke*'s right wrist with his right hand.
⑥ *Tori* grabs *uke*'s right elbow with his left hand while stepping in and pivoting on his left foot.
⑦–⑧ *Tori* controls *uke*'s elbow and wrist and pins him face down on the ground.

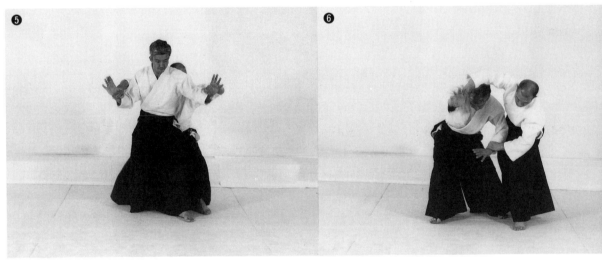

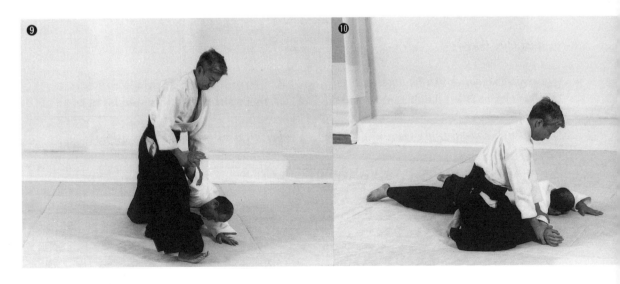

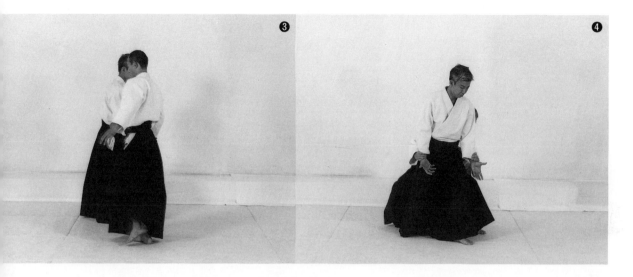

Ushiro Ryotekubi-dori Dai-Ikkyo

(*omote*)

① Assume a *migi-ai-hanmi* stance.

②–④ *Uke* approaches from the front, and moves around to grab *tori*'s wrists from behind. When his wrists are grabbed, *tori* takes a step forward on his left foot.

⑤ *Tori* raises his hands high.

⑥–⑦ *Tori* takes a step back on his left foot while cutting down with both hands.

⑧ *Tori* grabs *uke*'s right elbow with his left hand and his right wrist with his right hand.

⑨–⑩ *Tori* steps forward while controlling *uke*'s elbow and wrist and pins him face down on the ground.

In ⑦–⑧, keep a tight grip on your partner's elbow while rotating your hand to break his grip and then secure your own hold on his wrist.

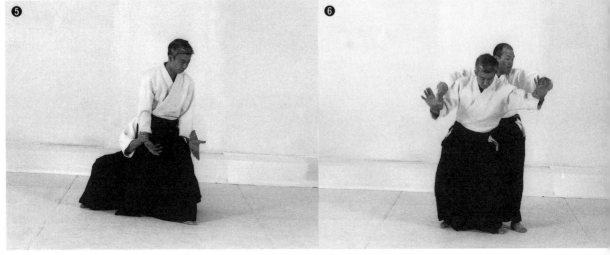

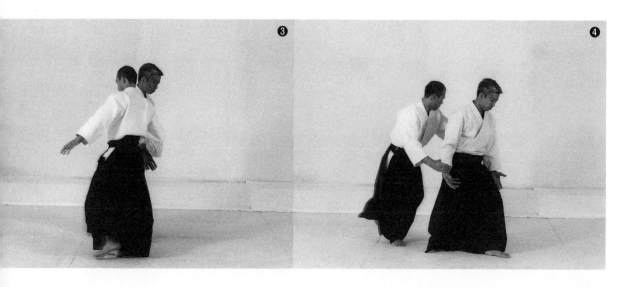

Ushiro Ryotekubi-dori Dai-Ikkyo
(*ura*)

① Assume a *migi-ai-hanmi* stance.

②–⑤ *Uke* approaches from the front, and moves around to grab *tori*'s wrists from behind. When his wrists are grabbed, *tori* takes a step forward on his left foot.

⑥ *Tori* raises both arms high.

⑦ *Tori* takes a step back on his left foot while cutting down with both hands.

⑧ *Tori* grabs *uke*'s elbow and wrist.

⑨–⑩ *Tori* steps further behind *uke* on his left foot and pivots.

⑪ *Tori* controls *uke*'s elbow and wrist and pins him face down on the ground.

2. DAI-NIKYO (KOTE-MAWASHI) (WRIST TURN)

The *dai-nikyo* pin is designed to develop flexibility of the shoulder, elbow, and especially the wrist. Both the *omote* and *ura* versions of this pin have many variations.

Shomen-uchi Dai-Nikyo

(*omote*)

① Assume a *migi-ai-hanmi* stance.

② When *uke* steps forward to deliver a *shomen* strike with his right hand-sword, *tori* takes a half-step in with his right foot and deflects the blow with both hand-swords.

③ *Tori* takes a big step in with his left foot while cutting down on *uke*'s right arm with both hands.

④ *Tori* grabs *uke*'s right elbow with his left hand and rotates his right hand to take hold of *uke*'s right wrist and the back of his hand.

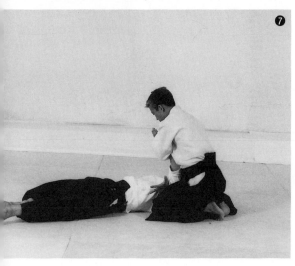

⑤–⑧ *Tori* steps forward and brings *uke* down to the ground.

⑦ *Tori* applies the *nikyo* pin to *uke*'s right shoulder, elbow, and wrist, pressing *uke*'s arm in the direction of his head.

Close-up of figure ⑦ from a different angle.

CHECKPOINT: In the *nikyo* pin, the palm of your left hand should be turned upward at your partner's wrist and your right hand-sword should control his elbow tightly against your body.

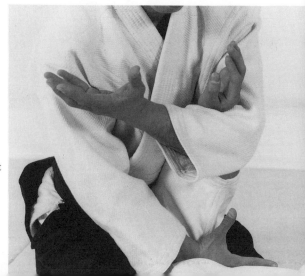

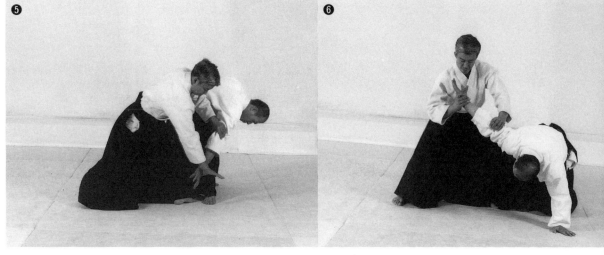

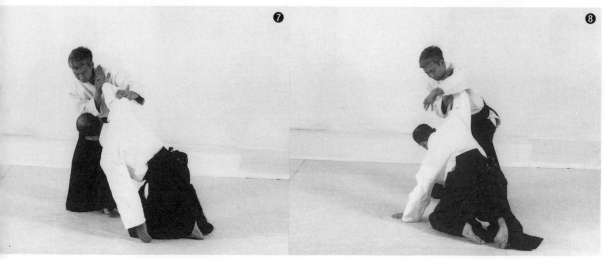

Shomen-uchi Dai-Nikyo (ura)

① Assume a *migi-ai-hanmi* stance.

② *Uke* steps forward to deliver a *shomen* strike with his right hand-sword.

③ *Tori* steps forward on his left foot to *uke*'s right side and controls the attacking arm with both hand-swords.

④–⑤ *Tori* pivots on the left foot while cutting down on *uke*'s arm and rotating his right hand.

⑥ *Tori* grabs *uke*'s right wrist and to the back of his hand.

⑦–⑨ *Tori* grabs *uke*'s right elbow with his left hand and applies the *nikyo* lock to *uke*'s right wrist with his right hand.

⑩ *Tori* presses down on *uke*'s shoulder, drops down to the ground, and turns on his left knee, bringing *uke* face down to the ground.

⑪ *Tori* applies the *nikyo* pin to *uke*'s right arm.

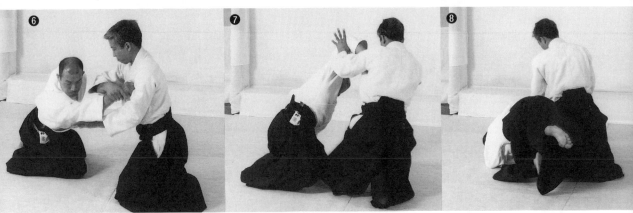

CHECKPOINT: Grab and control your partner's elbow from underneath. Grab his wrist tightly between your thumb and little finger.

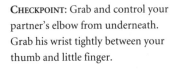

Close-up of figure ⑦ from a different angle.

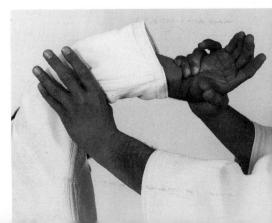

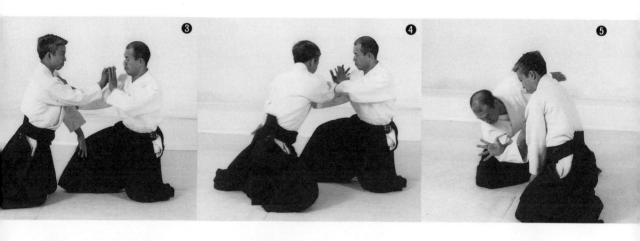

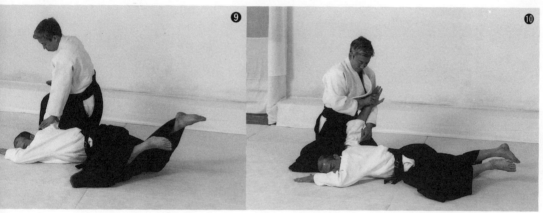

Kata-dori Dai-Nikyo (suwari-waza) (seated)

(*omote*)

①–② *Uke* slides forward to grab *tori*'s left shoulder with his right hand.

③ *Tori* applies *atemi* to *uke*'s face with his right fist.

④–⑤ *Tori* slides forward on his right knee while cutting down on *uke*'s right arm with his right hand-sword.

⑥–⑦ *Tori* grabs *uke*'s right wrist with his right hand, and pushes up on *uke*'s right elbow with his left hand.

⑧–⑨ *Tori* moves forward on his knees and brings *uke* face down to the ground.

⑩–⑪ *Tori* applies the *nikyo* pin.

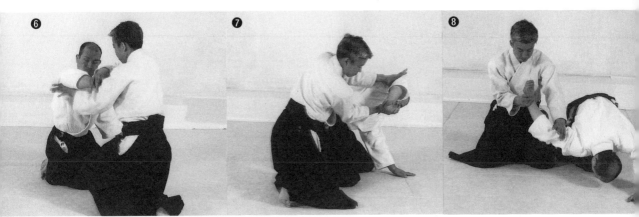

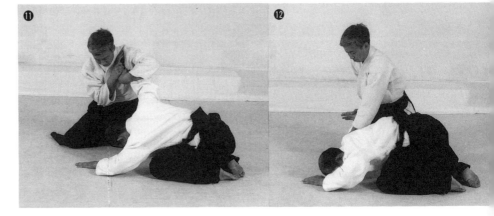

Kata-dori Dai-Nikyo (suwari-waza) (seated)
(ura)

①–② *Uke* slides forward to grab *tori*'s left shoulder with his right hand.

③ *Tori* applies *atemi* to *uke*'s face with his right fist.

④–⑤ *Tori* slides out to the left while cutting down on *uke*'s arm with his right hand-sword.

⑥–⑧ *Tori* grabs *uke*'s right wrist with his right hand and then pivots on his left knee while pressing down on *uke*'s right elbow with his left hand.

⑨–⑪ *Tori* applies the *nikyo* lock to *uke*'s right wrist, back of hand, and elbow.

⑫–⑬ *Tori* slides back on his left knee while pressing down on *uke*'s elbow, bringing him face down to the ground.

⑭ *Tori* applies the *nikyo* pin.

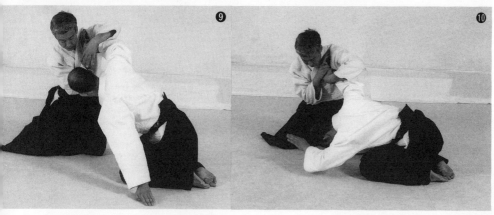

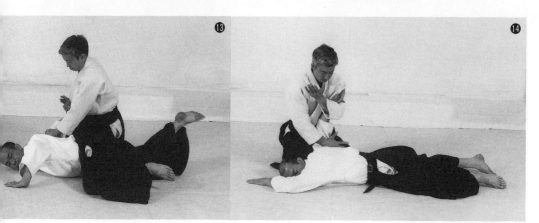

Close-up of figure ⑪ from a different angle.

CHECKPOINT: Use your right hand to turn your partner's wrist and back of hand while keeping your right arm close to your own body. Apply additional pressure with your left hand from above.

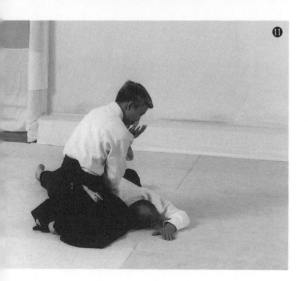

Katate-dori Dai-Nikyo (gyaku-hanmi) (*omote*)

① Assume a *hidari-gyaku-hanmi* stance.

② *Uke* grabs *tori*'s left wrist with his right hand.

③ *Tori* applies *atemi* to *uke*'s face with his right fist while stepping forward on his right foot.

④–⑤ *Tori* pivots on his right foot while cutting down on *uke*'s right arm with his right hand-sword.

⑥ *Tori* grabs *uke*'s right wrist with his right hand and pushes up on *uke*'s right elbow with his left hand.

⑦–⑨ *Tori* takes two big steps forward while pressing down on *uke*'s elbow, bringing him face down to the ground.

⑩–⑪ *Tori* applies the *nikyo* lock to *uke*'s right arm.

Katate-dori Dai-Nikyo (gyaku-hanmi)

(*ura*)

① Assume a *gyaku-hanmi* stance.

② *Uke* grabs *tori*'s left wrist with his right hand.

③ *Tori* applies *atemi* to *uke*'s face with his right fist.

④ *Tori* steps out to the left while cutting down on *uke*'s right arm with his right hand-sword.

⑤ *Tori* grabs *uke*'s right wrist with his right hand and uses his left hand to control *uke*'s right elbow.

⑥–⑦ *Tori* steps in on his left foot and sweeps around on his right foot while cutting down on *uke*'s arm.

⑧–⑨ *Tori* applies the *nikyo* lock to *uke*'s right wrist and back of hand and elbow.

⑩–⑪ *Tori* presses down on *uke*'s right elbow with his left hand while pivoting on his left foot, bringing him face down to the ground.

⑫ *Tori* applies the *nikyo* pin to *uke*'s shoulder.

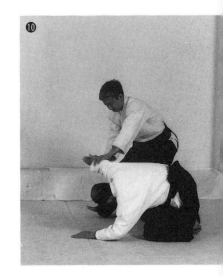

Ushiro Ryotekubi-dori Dai-Nikyo

(*omote*)

① Assume a *migi-ai-hanmi* stance.

②–⑤ *Uke* approaches from the front, and moves around to grab *tori*'s wrists from the back. When his wrists are grabbed, *tori* takes a step forward on his left foot.

⑥–⑦ *Tori* raises his arms, and then steps back on his left foot while cutting down with his hands.

⑧ *Tori* grabs *uke*'s right wrist with his right hand and *uke*'s right elbow with his left hand.

⑨–⑪ *Tori* steps forward and presses down on *uke*'s arm, bringing him face down to the ground.

⑫ *Tori* applies the *nikyo* pin to *uke*'s right arm.

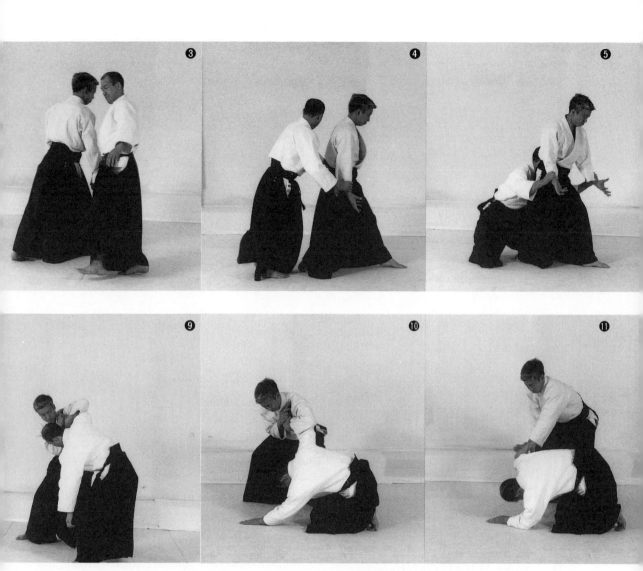

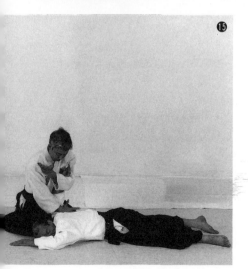

Ushiro Ryotekubi-dori Dai-Nikyo (*ura*)

① Assume a *migi-ai-hanmi* stance.

②–⑤ *Uke* approaches from the front and moves around to grab *tori*'s wrists from behind. When *tori*'s wrists are grabbed, he takes a step forward on his left foot.

⑥–⑦ *Tori* raises his arms and then steps back on his left foot while cutting down with both hands.

⑧ *Tori* grabs *uke*'s right wrist with his right hand and *uke*'s right elbow with his left hand while stepping in with his left foot.

⑨–⑩ *Tori* brings *uke*'s right wrist and back of hand to his left shoulder and applies the *nikyo* lock.

⑪–⑫ *Tori* presses down on *uke*'s right elbow while pivoting on his left foot, bringing *uke* face down to the ground.

⑬–⑮ *Tori* applies the *nikyo* to *uke*'s right shoulder as shown.

3. DAI-SANKYO (KOTE-HINERI) (WRIST TWIST)

The *dai-sankyo* lock and pin applies pressure to the shoulder, elbow, and wrist in a different manner than *dai-nikyo,* and it is executed according to *dai-ikkyo* principles. Please note the difference between the *dai-nikyo* and *dai-sankyo* finishing pin.

Shomen-uchi Dai-Sankyo (*suwari-waza*) (seated)

(*omote*)

① Sit in *seiza.*

② *Uke* moves forward to deliver a *shomen* strike with his right hand-sword.

③ *Tori* slides forward on his front knee and deflects the blow with both hand-swords.

④–⑤ *Tori* cuts down on *uke*'s arm with both hand-swords and grabs the outside of *uke*'s right hand.

⑥ *Tori* applies the *sankyo* lock and raises *uke*'s arm.

⑦–⑨ *Tori* steps forward on his right knee and uses his right hand to press down on *uke*'s right elbow, bringing him face down to the ground.

⑩–⑪ *Tori* applies the sankyo pin as shown.

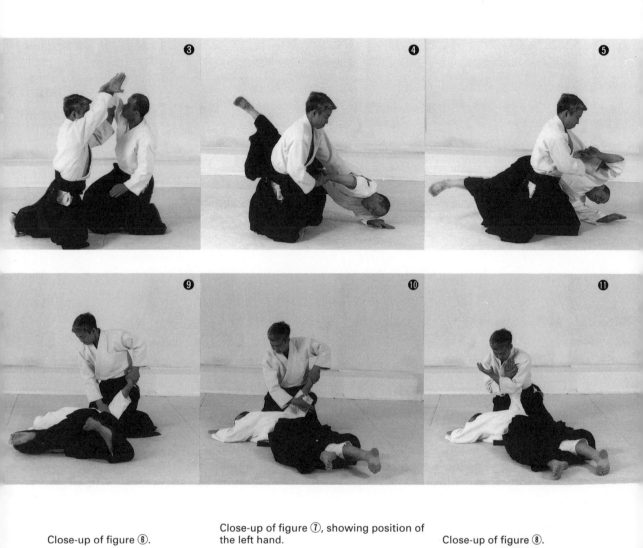

Close-up of figure ⑥.

Close-up of figure ⑦, showing position of the left hand.

Close-up of figure ⑧.

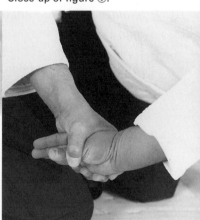

CHECKPOINT: Secure a tight grip with your little finger when applying the *sankyo* lock, and twist your partner's hand as shown here (⑥–⑧).

Shomen-uchi Dai-Sankyo (suwari-waza) (seated)
(*ura*)

① Sit in *seiza*.

② *Uke* slides forward to deliver a *shomen* strike with his right hand-sword.

③ *Tori* slides forward on his left knee to *uke*'s right side and controls the attacking arm with his hand-swords.

④ *Tori* pivots on his left knee and breaks *uke*'s posture.

⑤ *Tori* applies the *sankyo* lock to *uke*'s right wrist and back of hand.

⑥–⑦ *Tori* continues to turn while pressing down on *uke*'s elbow to bring him face down to the ground.

⑧–⑨ *Tori* applies the *sankyo* pin to *uke*'s right arm.

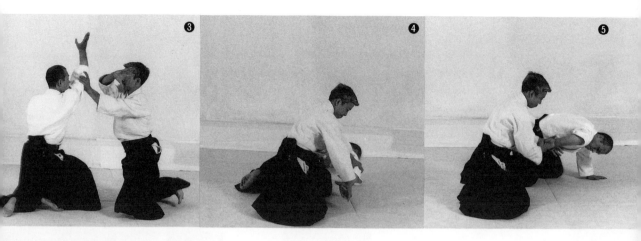

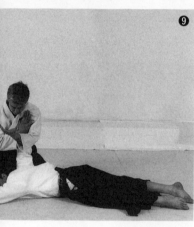

CHECKPOINT: Apply strong pressure to the back of your partner's hand with your right hand and keep your left palm upward, tight against his elbow, to control him completely.

Close-up of figure ⑨.

Katate-dori Dai-Sankyo (gyaku-hanmi)

(*omote: uchi-kaiten*)

1. Assume a *migi-gyaku-hanmi* stance.
2. *Uke* grabs *tori*'s right wrist with his left hand.
3. *Tori* applies *atemi* to *uke*'s face with his left fist while taking a step forward on his right foot.
4. – 5. *Tori* steps in on his left foot, pivots, and cuts down with his right hand-sword.
6. – 7. *Tori* releases *uke*'s grip, grabs *uke*'s left wrist and back of hand with his left hand, and applies the *sankyo* lock.
8. *Tori* steps out to the left while pressing down on *uke*'s left elbow.
9. – 10. *Tori* brings *uke* face down all the way to the ground.
11. *Tori* applies the *sankyo* pin to *uke*'s left shoulder.

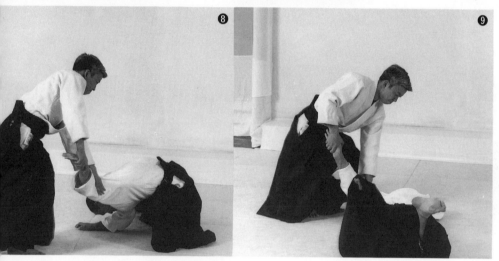

143

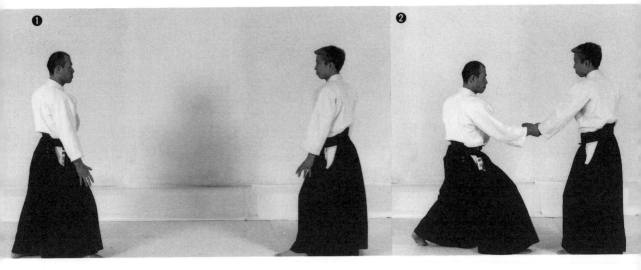

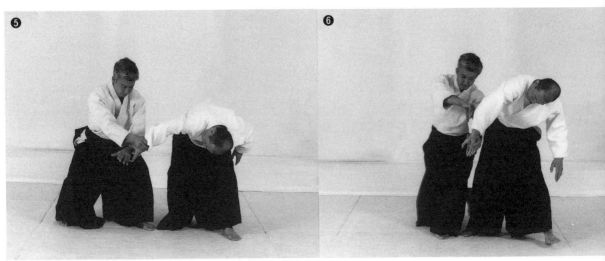

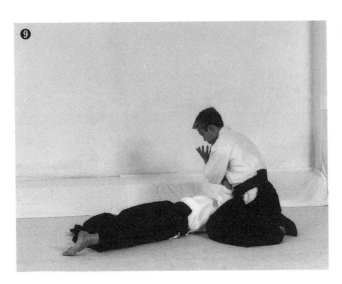

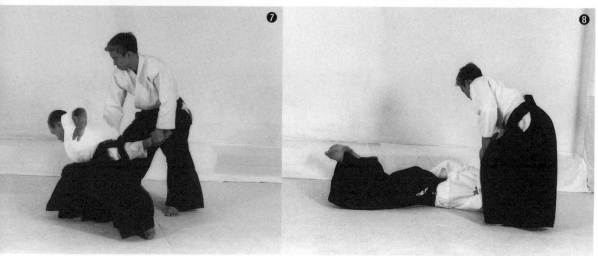

Katate-dori Dai-Sankyo (gyaku-hanmi)

(*ura: uchi-kaiten*)

① Assume a *hidari-gyaku-hanmi* stance.

② *Uke* grabs *tori*'s left wrist with his right hand.

③ *Tori* applies *atemi* to *uke*'s face with his right fist while taking a step forward on his left foot.

④ *Tori* steps in on his right foot and pivots while cutting down with his left hand-sword.

⑤ *Tori* releases *uke*'s grip and grabs *uke*'s right wrist and back of hand with his right hand.

⑥–⑦ *Tori* applies the *sankyo* lock to *uke*'s right hand and sweeps around with his right foot while pressing down on *uke*'s right elbow.

⑧ *Tori* brings *uke* face down to the ground.

⑨ *Tori* applies the *sankyo* lock to *uke*'s right arm.

Ushiro Ryotekubi-dori Dai-Sankyo (*omote*)

① Assume a *migi-ai-hanmi* stance.

②–⑤ *Uke* approaches from the front and moves around to grab *tori*'s wrists from behind. When *tori*'s wrists are grabbed he takes a step forward on his left foot.

⑥ *Tori* raises both arms high.

⑦ *Tori* takes a step back on his left foot while cutting down with both hands.

⑧ *Tori* releases *uke*'s grip and grabs *uke*'s right wrist and back of hand with his left hand.

⑨–⑩ *Tori* applies the *sankyo* lock to *uke*'s right hand while stepping out to the front with his right foot and pressing down on *uke*'s elbow.

⑪–⑫ *Tori* brings *uke* all the way face down to the ground.

⑬ *Tori* applies the *sankyo* pin to *uke*'s right shoulder.

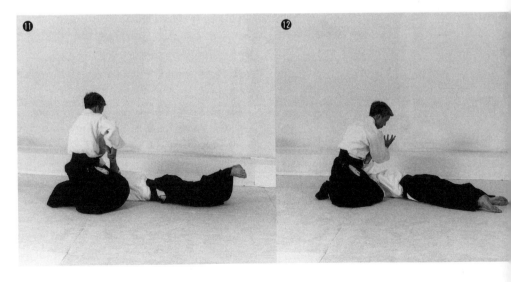

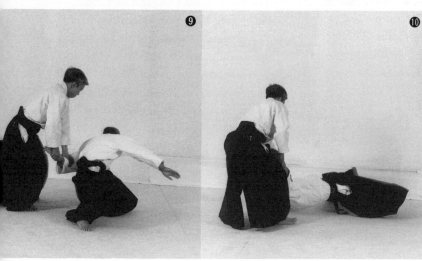

Close-up of figure ⑫ from a different angle.

Ushiro Ryotekubi-dori Dai-Sankyo (ura)

① Assume a *hidari-ai-hanmi* stance.

②–④ *Uke* approaches from the front and moves around to grab *tori*'s wrists from behind. When *tori*'s wrists are grabbed, he takes a step forward on his right foot.

⑤ *Tori* raises both arms high.

⑥ *Tori* steps back on his right foot and cuts down with both hands.

⑦ *Tori* releases *uke*'s grip and grabs *uke*'s left wrist and back of hand with his right hand.

⑧–⑨ *Tori* pivots to the rear while applying the *sankyo* lock to *uke*'s left hand with his right hand and pressing down on *uke*'s left elbow.

⑩–⑪ *Tori* brings *uke* face down all the way to the ground.

⑫ *Tori* applies the *sankyo* pin to *uke*'s left arm.

4. DAI-YONKYO (TEKUBI-OSAE) (WRIST PIN)

Dai-yonkyo is very similar in execution to *dai-ikkyo* with the added element of the application of strong pressure to the vital spots on your partner's wrist. *Dai-yonkyo* is not really a lock but rather a different form of controlling your partner. Pressure to the artery is applied in different places in the *omote* and *ura* variations.

Shomen-uchi Dai-Yonkyo (*omote*)

① Assume a *migi-ai-hanmi* stance.

② When *uke* steps forward to deliver a *shomen* strike with his right hand-sword, *tori* takes a half-step in with his right foot and deflects the blow with his hand-swords.

③ *Tori* grabs *uke*'s elbow and wrist and cuts down while stepping in with his left foot.

④–⑤ *Tori* takes two more steps forward bringing *uke* face down to the ground and applies *yonkyo* to *uke*'s wrist, concentrating his power at the base of his index finger and putting strong pressure on *uke*'s artery.

Shomen-uchi Dai-Yonkyo (*ura*)

① Assume a *migi-ai-hanmi* stance.

② When *uke* steps forward to deliver a *shomen* strike with his right hand-sword, *tori* steps in with his left foot to *uke*'s right side and deflects the attack with his hand-swords.

③–④ *Tori* pivots on his left foot while cutting down on *uke*'s right arm.

⑤–⑥ *Tori* holds *uke*'s right wrist with his right hand and applies *yonkyo* to the outside vital spot of *uke*'s wrist with his left hand while cutting down with a big sweep of his right leg.

⑦–⑧ *Tori* brings *uke* face down to the ground and pins him by applying *yonkyo* to his wrist as shown.

Showing the pin in figure
⑤ from a different angle.

Katate-dori Dai-Yonkyo (gyaku-hanmi)

(*omote*)

① Assume a *hidari-gyaku-hanmi* stance.

② *Uke* grabs *tori*'s left wrist with his right hand.

③–④ *Tori* steps forward on his right foot and pivots while cutting down on *uke*'s right arm with his right hand-sword.

⑤ *Tori* grabs *uke*'s right wrist with his right hand and *uke*'s elbow with his left hand.

⑥–⑧ *Tori* takes two big steps forward while cutting down on *uke*'s arm, bringing him face down to the ground.

⑨–⑩ *Tori* pins *uke*'s right arm by applying *yonkyo (omote)* to his right wrist.

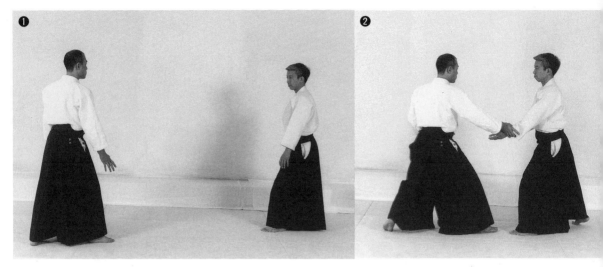

CHECKPOINT: Twist your partner's wrist to the inside by applying pressure to the vital spot on the outside of his wrist with the base of your index finger.

Detail of figure ⑨ from a different angle (cloe-up).

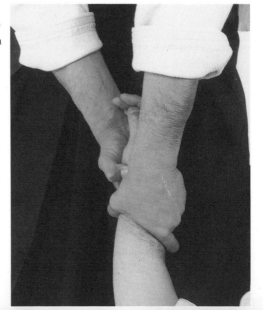

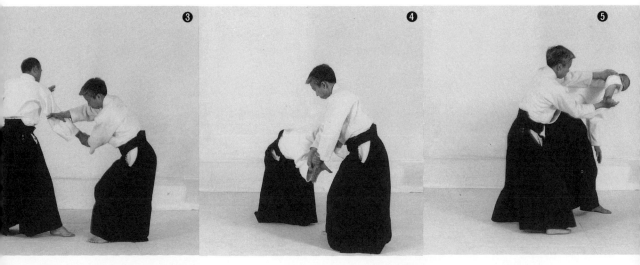

Showing the pin in of figure ⑨ from a different angle.

Katate-dori Dai-Yonkyo (gyaku-hanmi)

(*ura*)

① Assume a *hidari-gyaku-hanmi* stance.

② *Uke* grabs *tori*'s right wrist with his left hand.

③–④ *Tori* steps out to the side on his left foot while cutting down on *uke*'s arm with his right hand-sword.

⑤ *Tori* grabs *uke*'s right wrist with his right hand and *uke*'s elbow with his left hand while stepping to the back.

⑥ *Tori* pivots on his left foot while cutting down on *uke*'s arm.

⑦ *Tori* applies *yonkyo* to *uke*'s right wrist.

⑧ *Tori* pivots on his left foot while cutting down on *uke*'s right arm, bringing him face down to the ground.

⑨ *Tori* pins *uke* by applying *yonkyo* to his wrist.

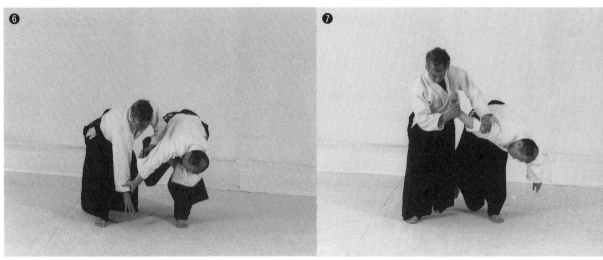

Close-up of figure ⑧ from a different angle.

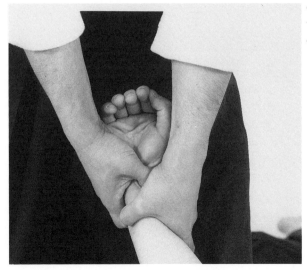

CHECKPOINT: Apply the *yonkyo* hold by using the base of your index finger to put pressure on your partner's artery.

Ushiro Ryotekubi-dori Dai-Yonkyo

(*omote*)

① Assume a *migi-ai-hanmi* stance.

②–④ *Uke* approaches from the front and moves behind *tori* to grab his wrists from behind. When *tori*'s wrists are grabbed, he takes a step forward on his left foot.

⑤ *Tori* raises both arms high.

⑥ *Tori* takes a step back on his left foot while cutting down with both hands.

⑦ *Tori* grabs *uke*'s right wrist with his right hand and *uke*'s right elbow with his left hand.

⑧–⑨ *Tori* steps forward while pressing down on *uke*'s arm, bringing him face down all the way to the ground. *Tori* completes the pin by applying *yonkyo* to *uke*'s right wrist.

Ushiro Ryotekubi-dori Dai-Yonkyo

(*ura*)

① Assume a *hidari-ai-hanmi* stance.

②–⑤ *Uke* approaches from the front and moves around to grab *tori*'s wrists from behind. When *tori*'s wrists are grabbed, he takes a step forward on his right foot.

⑥ *Tori* raises both arms high.

⑦ *Tori* takes a step back on his right foot while cutting down with both hands.

⑧–⑨ *Tori* grasps *uke*'s left elbow with his right hand and *uke*'s left wrist with his left hand.

⑩–⑫ *Tori* applies *yonkyo* (*ura*) to *uke*'s left wrist and pivots on his right foot while cutting down.

⑬–⑭ *Tori* brings *uke* face down to the ground and applies *yonkyo* to *uke*'s left wrist to complete the pin.

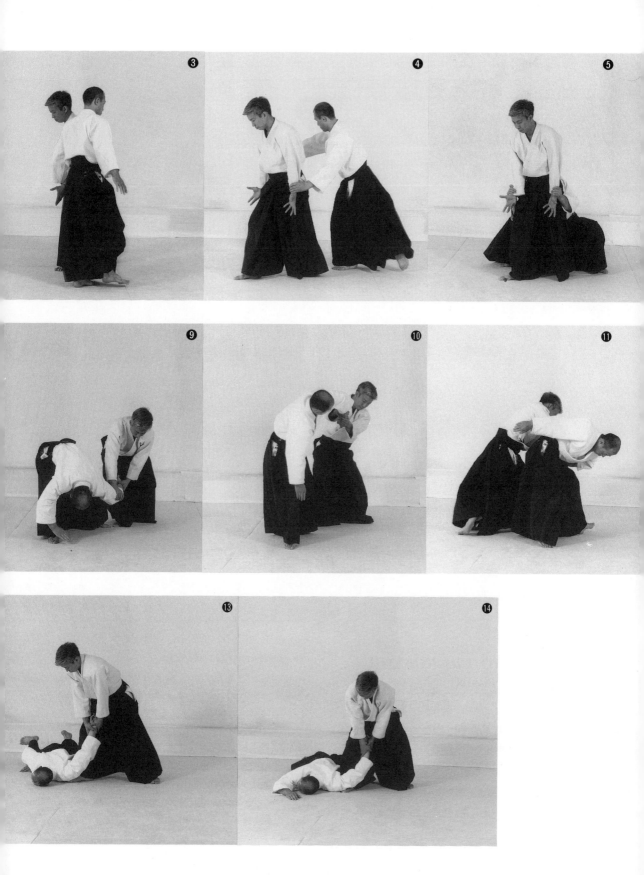

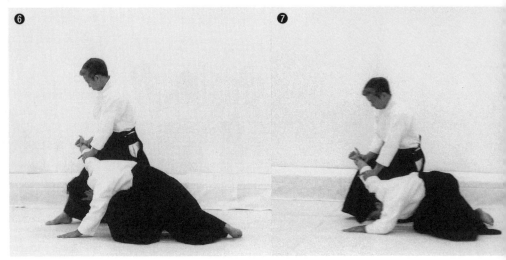

5. DAI-GOKYO (UDE-NOBASHI) (ARM EXTENSION)

Dai-gokyo was originally designed as a defense against a knife attack. The attacker was brought face down to the ground and the knife taken away. In regular practice, however, the knife is imaginary.

Shomen-uchi Dai-Gokyo
(*omote*)

①–② When *uke* delivers a *shomen* strike from a *migi-ai-hanmi* stance, *tori* steps forward and controls *uke*'s right elbow with both hands.

③ *Tori* grabs *uke*'s right wrist from underneath.

④–⑧ *Tori* steps forward while controlling *uke*'s right elbow and wrist and cutting down all the way to the ground.

⑨ *Tori* applies the *gokyo* pin to *uke*'s right elbow and wrist as shown.

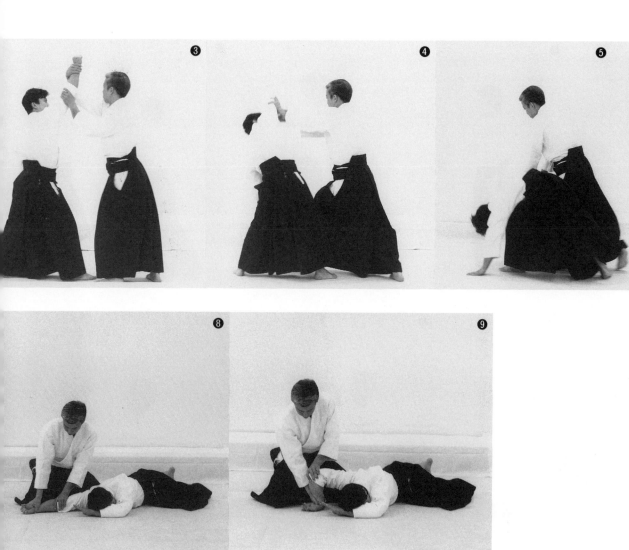

CHECKPOINT: Grab your partner's elbow from underneath and use your little finger to secure a firm grip on his wrist as you turn his hand away from you.

Close-up of figure ③.

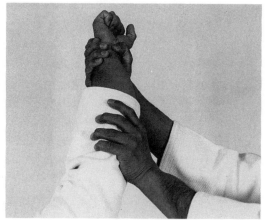

Shomen-uchi Dai-Gokyo (ura)

①–③ When *uke* delivers a *shomen* strike from a *migi-ai-hanmi* stance, *tori* steps forward on his left foot to *uke*'s right side while deflecting the blow with both hands.

④ *Tori* grabs *uke*'s right wrist from underneath with his right hand.

⑤–⑦ *Tori* pivots on his left foot while cutting down on *uke*'s arm.

Close-up of figure ③.

Close-up of figure ⑨, from a different angle.

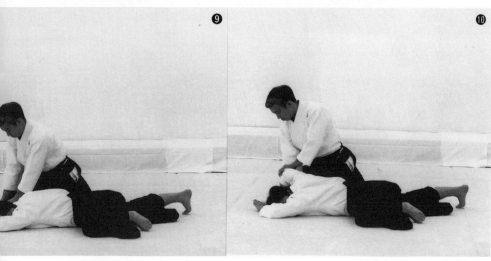

⑧–⑩ *Tori* brings *uke* all the way down to the
ground and applies the *gokyo* pin to *uke*'s
right elbow and arm.

Close-up of figure ⑩,
from a different angle.

Figure ⑩, showing the concluding pin
directly from the front.

CHECKPOINT: Push your partner's elbow
back from underneath to direct the attack
away from you. Use the little finger of
your left hand to secure a good grip on
his elbow, slide in on your right knee, and
pin his right hand by holding his thumb
with the base of your index finger. Raise
up his elbow with your left hand and
bend his wrist more than 90 degrees.

Yokomen-uchi Dai-Gokyo (*omote*)

① From a *hidari-ai-hanmi* stance, *uke* steps in on his right
   foot and delivers a *yokomen* attack with his right fist.

②–③ *Tori* steps forward on his left foot and deflects the blow
   with his left hand-sword while applying *atemi* with his
   right hand-sword to *uke*'s face.

④ *Tori* grabs *uke*'s right wrist from underneath.

⑤–⑧ *Tori* pushes up on *uke*'s right elbow with his left hand
   and then steps forward while pressing down on *uke*'s
   arm to bring him down to the ground.

⑨ *Tori* applies the *gokyo* pin to *uke*'s elbow and wrist.

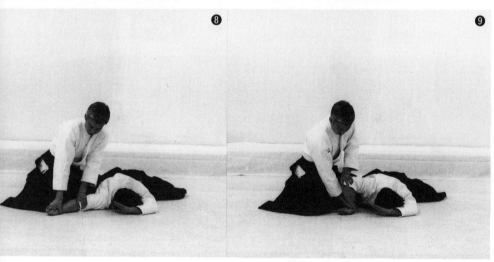

Good example for figure ③.   Bad example for figure ③.

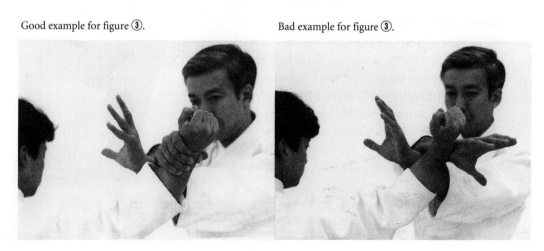

Yokomen-uchi Dai-Gokyo (ura)

① From a *hidari-ai-hanmi* stance, *uke* steps forward on his right foot to deliver a *yokomen* strike with his right fist.

② *Tori* steps forward on his left foot and deflects the attack with his left hand-sword while applying *atemi* with his right hand-sword to *uke*'s face.

③ *Tori* grabs *uke*'s right wrist from underneath with his right hand.

④–⑦ *Tori* pivots on his left foot while cutting down on *uke*'s right arm.

⑧–⑨ *Tori* brings *uke* face down all the way to the ground.

⑩ *Tori* applies the *gokyo* pin to *uke*'s right arm.

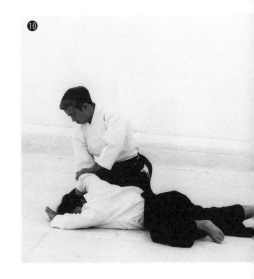

CHECKPOINT: Hold your partner's elbow tightly with your left hand, and bend his wrist more than 90 degrees.

Close-up of figure ⑩ from a different angle.

Dai-Ikkyo

Dai-Nikyo

Kaiten-nage

Shiho-nage

Tenchi-nage

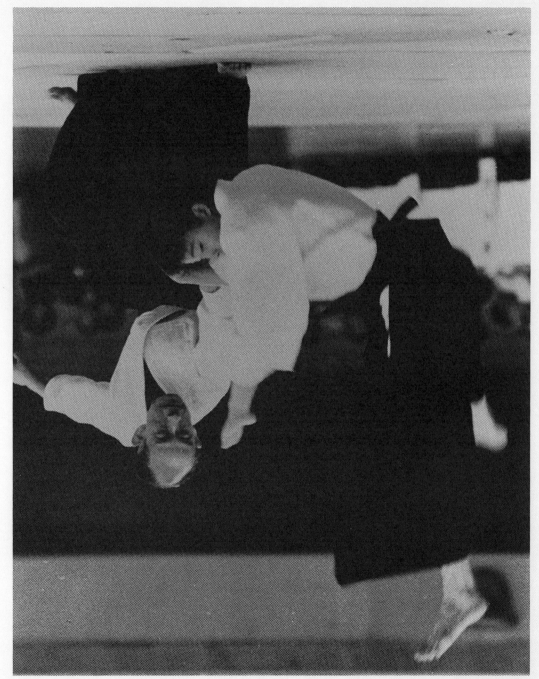

Tori: Kisshomaru Ueshiba; *uke:* Moriteru Ueshiba, in a 1974 exhibition.